DAMIEN,
the Leper Priest

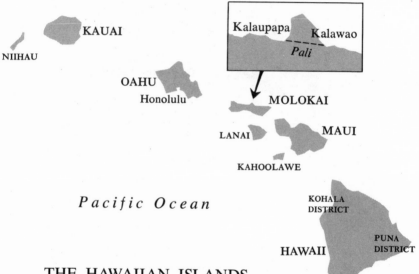

KAUAI

NIIHAU

Kalaupapa Kalawao

Pali

OAHU

Honolulu

MOLOKAI

LANAI

MAUI

KAHOOLAWE

Pacific Ocean

KOHALA
DISTRICT

PUNA
DISTRICT

HAWAII

THE HAWAIIAN ISLANDS

Anne E. Neimark

DAMIEN, the Leper Priest

William Morrow and Company • New York
1980

By the Same Author
With This Gift, The Story of Edgar Cayce

1 2 3 4 5 6 7 8 9 10

Library of Congress Cataloging in Publication Data
Neimark, Anne E.
    Damien, the leper priest.
    Summary: A biography of the heroic priest who gave his life working for the lepers in the Hawaiian Islands.
    1. Damien, Father, 1840-1889—Juvenile Literature. 2. Catholic Church—Clergy—Biography—Juvenile literature. 3. Clergy—Hawaii—Biography—Juvenile literature. 4. Missionaries—Hawaii—Biography—Juvenile literature. 5. Missionaries—Belgium—Biography—Juvenile literature. [1. Damien, Father, 1840-1889. 2. Missionaries] I. Title.
BX4705.D25N44   266'.2'092'4   [B]   [92]   80-15141
ISBN 0-688-22246-3   ISBN 0-688-32246-8 (lib. bdg.)

To my friend Tom Kamin,
because it matters.

You are that miracle
Surprising lone wanderers in the wilderness

—Rainer Maria Rilke

DAMIEN,
the Leper Priest

Chapter

The Belgian countryside was painted by a thick wash of fog. Limbs of evergreens dipped like brushes into the river Dyle, and roads meandered along fields of potatoes, beans, asparagus, and beets. The northern region of Flanders was a land of rugged peasants, of men who toiled over crops, of women who labored over children and chores.

Here, at the small hamlet of Tremeloo, farmhouses lay under thatched roofs and roadside religious shrines dotted the pathways. And here, on January 3, 1840, was born the seventh of eight children to Frans and Anne-Catherine de Veuster, a son who was baptized with the name of Joseph but who one day would be known to the world as Damien.

Joseph de Veuster grew into boyhood against the somber colors of his native land. Gray fogs obscured the river where he learned to skate boldly on winter ice. The greens and browns of the earth changed texture and hue as year by year he learned to pit his budding strength against the rigors of his father's farm. At *kermesses*, the country fairs, Joseph stared in wonder at the rainbow colors on the wooden stalls, the baskets brimming with ripened vegetables and fruit, with the tinted wax of candles, with the shiny clay vases and bowls that had been baked in fiery kilns.

On most afternoons, Joseph raced the two miles home from school at nearby Werchter, leaving brothers or sisters huffing breathlessly behind. The red-brick house where the family lived stood apart from a barn where chickens scratched in the yard. Joseph's mother cleaned the tiled kitchen, occasionally stirring stew or broth on the stove. There Joseph and his brother Auguste and his sister Pauline would

12

ask her to read to them. Aside from the Bible, a single book was kept in the house—a two-foot-high old volume with crude woodcuts, printed in Flemish in Gothic letters, and entitled *The Lives of the Saints*.

When Anne-Catherine de Veuster sat down in a chair, the children gathered around and put the book in her lap. Wide-eyed, they listened to the glorious tales of martyrs and hermits who had given their lives to great missions or causes. After the stories were read, and while two older brothers, Léonce and Gérard, worked in the fields, Joseph invented games to play with Auguste and Pauline. All three might become armored knights of olden times, or stoic missionaries, or brave crusaders.

Sacrifice was blended into the soil of the Belgian farm country. Survival upon the land demanded resilience and fortitude, and the Catholic church reaped the benefits in its pious, devoted congregations. At the age of six, Joseph had been taken by an uncle on a rattling market wagon to the city of Mechlin. There the boy saw a requiem high mass for Pope Gregory XVI. Bishops and priests knelt silently in prayer, lighted candles reflected the pomp and glory, and Joseph's small fist gripped his rosary tightly.

Yet he was not a child who easily yielded himself

13

to a discipline or who always did what he was told. Something rebellious and daring stirred in him, an energy that was never to be contained. At eight years old, he once persuaded four of his sisters and brothers to play hooky from school with him. Joseph instructed them to kneel mutely in a patch of bushes, where they spent the entire day being "hermits." Not until sundown, when they still had not spoken a word to each other, were they discovered by a search party of worried relatives.

Joseph liked to be alone and in silence. From his mother's Flemish book of tales, he remembered the stories of the ancient hermits, Antony and Paul, and he used to wander off pensively to tend sheep in the pastures, isolated from the company of others. Hours would pass as he perched on a grassy knoll, and he was nicknamed *le petit berger*, "the little shepherd," by neighboring farmers.

On other days, however, Joseph tried out a dangerous prank that had made him the envy of the boys in Tremeloo. Hiding a school friend behind a roadside tree, he waited for a passing market wagon, and when one clattered by, he signaled his friend to toss a handful of rocks onto the road. The impact of stones startled the driver into loosening rein, and the horse broke into a wild, tumultuous gallop, but not before Joseph had jumped up and grabbed onto the splintery rear of the wagon.

14

Unchecked, the horse carried both driver and stowaway on a convulsive journey down the country road. Only the grip of Joseph's fingers held him free of the whirling stones and dirt beneath him. But, somehow, he was not afraid. His hair fanning out from his head, he swung precariously in the air, delighted by the risk of his adventure.

The driver was never pleased by this unsettling ride. Angry shouts echoed across the fields, and at length the steaming horse was reined in to a halt. The driver, whip held aloft, leaped from his seat and dashed after the black-haired young imp who'd "done it again." But Joseph, covering his face to avoid recognition, and weaving between trees or rolling down a ravine, always managed to escape being caught. The fog enfolded him or the evergreens shielded him, and he raced along the river toward the boundaries of his father's farm, his school friend trailing in his wake like a lumbering shadow.

By the time he was thirteen, Joseph was remarkably strong. His shoulders had widened and his arms and legs were firmly muscled. His eyes seemed to flame darkly but steadily under the black curls of his hair. Schooling at Werchter had ended, and he'd gone to work for his father. On the farm, he plowed, planted, harvested, tended the animals, built wagons, carts, and sheds, and trimmed trees. He also helped

15

the local smithy, learning to handle a hot iron and other blacksmith's tools. These tasks were ones any peasant boy might perform, but Joseph's strength was uncommon. By age fifteen, he could lift two-hundred-pound sacks of grain as if they were empty, a feat continually marveled at by the villagers.

Frans de Veuster, Joseph's father, had chosen the occupations for each of his children. His eldest daughter, Eugenie, had become an Ursuline nun but had died of typhus. Constance had married, and Pauline, four years older than Joseph, was sent to take Eugenie's place. Mary was at home, and Léonce and Gérard worked the farm, but Auguste also showed leanings toward the religious life. He was permitted to enter the Congregation of the Sacred Hearts, a small Catholic missionary order in nearby Louvain, which had been founded in the early 1800's by Father Coudrin, a French priest.

For Joseph, Frans de Veuster had more worldly plans. Frans himself dealt in grain, as well as running the farm. Several times a week he traveled on business to the teeming markets of Louvain, Mechlin, Antwerp, and Brussels. Commerce was flourishing in Belgium under King Leopold I, and Frans decided that his son Joseph should become a grain merchant.

Although the tuition was a burden on the family,

16

Joseph was sent South to attend commercial school at Braine-le-Comte. He would need to be fluent in both the languages of Belgium: his own Flemish, spoken in Flanders in the North, and the French of the Walloons in the South. Joseph did not, at first, question his father's plans. At Braine-le-Comte, he found himself memorizing columns of numbers and straining to comprehend lists of strange words. But although he had seen the grain market at Mechlin once with his uncle, he remembered more clearly the city's Cathedral of St. Rombaut, where he'd watched the requiem high mass for Pope Gregory XVI. He tried to concentrate more patiently on school. His letters home were saved by his family. "I talk to the Walloons a little," he wrote his mother and father. "All in the house is very clean and comfortable; our table is something like the one at an annual fair. . . ."

Many of the Walloon students made fun of Joseph because he was from Flanders and spoke in Flemish. Yet he did not remain the victim. "Any Walloons that laugh at me," he wrote his parents, "I hit with a ruler. . . . The first day I was a little shy, and I didn't like to ask for anything, though I had neither books, pens, paper, or anything I wanted. Afterwards I asked Mr. Derne, our master, for some books, a brush, some pens, and some copybooks.

On Sunday we went for a walk. I walked with a Walloon, and talked to him the whole time, and asked the name of everything I saw."

School gradually became routine to Joseph, and for two years he lived at Braine-le-Comte. Whenever he had free time, however, he took long walks by himself, seeking more open spaces. How good it was to gaze upward toward the boundless blue of the heavens. He was almost eighteen when special religious services were held by the congregation of Redemptorist Fathers in a local parish church. At night, Joseph attended services, drawn to the mysteries of the altar and to the golden tabernacle that housed the wafer and wine, symbols of the body and blood of Jesus Christ.

Visions of that tabernacle and altar embedded themselves in Joseph's thoughts. Back at school, after the final service, he knelt in prayer on the floorboards by his bed. Lists of words and columns of numbers were suddenly erased, and the lure of crusades, of missions to foreign lands, burned anew inside him.

Still, several months passed before he had come to a decision. He did not want to be a grain merchant or a farmer. He did not want an ordinary life. In spite of love for his earthly father, he would submit to the authority of the universal Father. He was

18

being called to another home from which he would never stray.

Letters to Tremeloo poured from him. He thanked his parents for sending him, at hardship to themselves, to school at Braine-le-Comte. Yet he wished to be part of the religious life. He wished it even if he were not learned enough to become a priest. He'd considered joining the Trappist monks, but his brother Auguste—having taken the name Pamphile at the Congregation of the Sacred Hearts—convinced him to come to Louvain for teaching or missionary work. "Would it not be possible," Joseph wrote his stunned parents, "for me to follow my brother Pamphile? I beg you to agree. . . ." And then, risking his father's anger as he had risked himself on the daring wagon rides in Tremeloo, he added, "I cannot imagine that you will hinder me. Such a mistake would make me eternally unhappy."

Frans and Anne-Catherine de Veuster consulted a local priest. If their son continued in his desire for religion, they were told, no one should deter him. And Joseph's letters did not veer from their single theme. So on a January morning in 1859, Frans regretfully laid aside his plans for his youngest son. In his Sunday suit and coat he rode from Tremeloo by horse and wagon and surprised Joseph at Braine-le-Comte, signing the boy out for a student absence.

Gruffly Frans remarked to Joseph that he had business to conduct in Louvain and would leave him for the day with his brother. Not another word was uttered between them about the future. Rime ice glazed the barren tree branches and the horse was breathing in short heaves when Joseph was deposited on the doorstep of the Sacred Hearts Monastery. His father immediately rode off across the square, and he was alone. Shivering, he read the metal wall plaque on the building: *Congregation of the Sacred Hearts of Jesus and Mary and of Perpetual Adoration of the Most Blessed Sacrament of the Altar.* His heart pounding with the moment of decision before him, Joseph lifted the door knocker and let it fall. When the black-robed priest who greeted him summoned Pamphile downstairs, he was grateful.

The two brothers were overjoyed to see each other. They walked side by side into the chapel to pray before the altar. In the sparkling light filtering through the stained-glass windows, Joseph asked Pamphile if he could possibly remain at the monastery. Perhaps he could, Pamphile replied. He would try to arrange an interview with the superior, Father Wencelas Vincke.

An hour later the interview was conducted in a long, low-ceilinged room graced by a large crucifix on a whitewashed wall. Joseph, his face flushed, was received by Father Vincke, and he introduced himself as Joseph de Veuster, age nineteen, of Tremeloo. He answered the superior's questions, frankly admitting to his brief schooling and to his lack of book knowledge. He did not attempt to make himself seem anything but what he was—a Belgian peasant, a son of the soil—but his dark eyes glowed and his breath came fast as he talked of committing himself to Christ and to the ideals of the congregation.

Father Vincke looked sternly at the younger brother of his novice, Pamphile. How very different the two were. Pamphile was slender, scholarly, having been taught the classics at the University of Louvain. This Joseph de Veuster was energetic and stocky, almost brash in his manner. By the standards of the congregation, he was past the best age to enter monastic life. The material world clung too closely to him, and besides he had not been properly educated. He was totally ignorant of Latin.

Yet, there was something, some force, some intensity, beyond the obvious physical strength that would fit him so well for grueling missionary work. The young Belgian's ardor was impressive. He could not be a priest without Latin, but he might be a lay brother. He could attend to the care of chapels and learn to teach the Bible. Father Vincke inclined his head in a slight nod of acknowledgment. Joseph de Veuster had been accepted.

That evening, when his father returned to the

monastery, Joseph stood squarely in the shadows beside Pamphile. He would not, he explained, be returning to school at Braine-le-Comte. He would not be working the farm in Tremeloo. Whatever disappointment he caused his parents, he was now entered as a postulant of the Sacred Hearts Congregation. He and Pamphile would live together at the monastery. He could not be a grain merchant. He was sorry, he said, but not for himself. He had discovered his life's vocation, and he must follow it.

Frans de Veuster did not evidence any emotion. Stiffly he touched Joseph on the shoulder and glanced at Pamphile. Then, turning to walk down the monastery steps toward his waiting market wagon, he pushed a crumpled pile of receipts from his grain sales into the pocket of his winter coat. Vesper bells were chiming overhead. Fervently Joseph called good-bye to his father, but Frans de Veuster did not address himself to the second youngest of his children. Resigned to the deed already accomplished—to his son's daring to choose his own way—the father stepped onto the ice-lacquered pavement in Louvain and pronounced softly, "It must be God's will."

Chapter **2**

The stillness of the monastery was almost palpable.
Joseph walked the halls and heard only the sound
of his own footsteps. Voices, if they drifted from the
dining room or rose across the chapel doorway, were
temperate and hushed. The stillness felt comfortable
to Joseph, yet it was a constraint on his abundant
energy. At times, he wanted to run and not walk,
to climb and not sit. He might speak too loudly with-

out noticing or clatter his dishes on a table. To remind himself of the teachings of the congregation, he'd taken a jackknife and carved into the lid of his study desk the words *Silence, Recollection,* and *Prayer.* His novice master hastily reproached him for this act. Joseph would do better, the novice master said, not to deface the furniture and to carve the words, instead, into the recesses of his heart.

Sometimes Joseph's peasant sturdiness was a boon to the congregation. A building had been purchased next door and was to be rebuilt as a chapel. In one room, a tall chimney tottered unsteadily on its foundation, but a crew of workmen refused to tear it down. The street was too crowded to use explosives, and the chimney too shaky for the men to scale ladders to dismantle it. No one seemed to have a solution, until Joseph came strolling by.

Quickly he surveyed the situation. Then with one hand he picked up a ladder and leaned it against the chimney. In spite of the scorn from the crewmen and concern from the priests and lay brothers who collected nearby, Joseph tucked a hammer in his belt and climbed the rungs of the ladder. While the chimneytop swayed and the onlookers gasped, he began hammering the bricks loose and dropping them onto a cloth. He did not pause in his efforts until the entire chimney was gone and the crewmen

24

were sent grumbling and muttering to an easier job.

In the sleeping quarters of the monastery, Joseph had been assigned a room with Pamphile. One night the elder brother awakened and found the younger asleep and unblanketed on the hardwood floor, denying himself bodily comfort in a practice called "mortification of the flesh." Pamphile nudged Joseph and urged him back to bed. The superior frowned on such practices, Pamphile explained. Whispering together, the two brothers pondered how best to make use of their earthly lives. The Congregation of the Sacred Hearts of Jesus and Mary contained several hundred members and had organized dangerous missions on foreign shores. The motherhouse was located in Paris, and missions operated in the Sandwich Islands of the South Seas, or Oceania, and in Peru, the Marquesas, and the Gambier Islands. Pamphile and Joseph both admired the courage of the missionary priests. In daylight, they would pray before an arched window painted with a likeness of St. Francis Xavier, the brave missionary explorer of the sixteenth century.

Several months after joining the congregation, Joseph persuaded Pamphile to teach him Latin vocabulary. Words and grammatical construction were exchanged in their late night talks, yet what started as simple, curious questioning soon was serious business. Joseph applied himself with such diligence to learning the language that, within six months, he could translate easily from many texts.

He was, in that winter, no longer referred to as Joseph de Veuster. Soon after his arrival, he had been issued the black cassock, or habit, of the congregation and was asked to assume his new name as a religious. He chose the name Damien, a decision that was unknowingly prophetic. The Damien who'd inspired him was a fourth-century French saint and physician who refused payment for treating the ill and willingly accepted a martyr's death.

It was from Damien then, not from Joseph, that letters were sent to Tremeloo. And it was Damien, not Joseph, whom Father Vincke reassessed as suitable for the priesthood. When he could translate the scholarly work of Cornelius Nepos, the Roman historian, Damien de Veuster was entered by his superior into preparation for priestly vows. He took the beginning vows of poverty, chastity, and obedience on October 7, 1860, and that autumn was transferred to study in Paris at the motherhouse on 31 rue de Picpus.

Ensconced in the bustling, sophisticated city, Damien remained cloistered from worldly concerns. He was instructed daily in philosophy, theology, and Greek. News of construction on the boulevards by the river Seine or of matinees by Sarah Bernhardt at the theater near the congregation barely filtered past the outside gate. "As I do not read the paper," he wrote his parents, "I am not well up in the state of affairs. It is very seldom I go out in the town."

This letter of Damien's from Paris described the arrival of the missionary bishops and the occasion of a pontifical mass in the Picpus chapel. "It was on Easter Sunday," Damien wrote. "Instead of two or three priests, twenty or twenty-five were at the altar. In the evening, after Vespers, the chapel was full of soldiers. The good bishop held a short discourse, gave them his blessing, and then came benediction. The soldiers sang, and served at the altar, in fact they did everything. They themselves were delighted. I believe this zealous missioner will shortly return to his mission in Oceania, and may possibly take some of us with him. Would you not be happy if I were to be one? . . . Good-bye, my dear parents. I commend myself to your charitable prayers."

The missionary bishops had sketched a vivid picture of serving in far-off lands. How urgent the need was, they said, for creating good works. The islands of the South Seas were fragrant and exotic, palm trees burgeoning like green parasols and flowers blooming in vibrant colors, but the natives were beset by illness and debauchery that could be blamed on white sailors from foreign ships.

Damien returned to Louvain in the fall of 1861,

27

consumed now by the desire for a missionary life. His hours of studying had caused him to wear thick, wire-rimmed spectacles, but he was twenty-one years old and at the prime of his strength. He ached to test himself, to overcome the resistance of body, soul, or mind. He wanted what was difficult, what might even be impossible. He longed for his own turn to live *The Imitation of Christ*, the book in the congregation library that prescribed the standard of Catholic behavior. In childhood, playing out the tales read to him by his mother, he had turned the family farmyard into a Holy Land in his imagination. Brave knights had battled savage Saracens; the Crusades were triumphantly revived. At the monastery, he still dreamed of battle, but of a more exacting struggle of believer against heathen, of good against evil, of emotional or physical health against the ravages of disease.

Before Damien could take part in any battles, however, Pamphile achieved a long-desired goal. The elder brother's studies were complete, and he was to conduct his first Mass as an ordained priest. Eight relatives escorted Frans and Anne-Catherine de Veuster to Louvain to watch Pamphile and Damien—once Auguste and Joseph—participate in the solemn ceremony. The monastery chapel was darkened, and candle flames were reflected in kaleidoscopic patterns on lofty windows. Pamphile, the new priest, stood at the altar and chanted aloud the traditional words, *"Benedicamus Domino."* Damien, the brother following in Pamphile's footsteps but not yet a priest himself, knelt before the altar and responded in a resonant voice, *"Deo gratias."*

By the summer of 1863, although Damien was studying advanced theology at the University of Louvain, he wrote home that he would not be a contributor to Catholic doctrine or theory. He accepted what he read but did not see himself as a scholar like his brother. In fact, his studies were almost forgotten when he heard that Bishop Maigret, stationed in Honolulu on the island of Oahu, had written to Father Vincke pleading for more missionaries. A few members of the congregation were to be chosen by the superior general at the motherhouse in Paris. They would be sent to join Bishop Maigret in the Sandwich Islands where they might bring the promise of a sanctified life to the untutored natives.

Damien waited for the list of future missionaries to arrive from 31 rue de Picpus. The hours he'd spent with the visiting bishops shimmered like a radiant ribbon through his dreaming. He could hardly bear to admit to himself how desperately he wished to be chosen for the mission to the Sandwich

Islands. His temper flared at mealtimes, and then he apologized to anyone who'd borne the brunt of it. Finally the decision was delivered to Louvain. Yes, the superior general said, the mission in Oceania would be enlarged. Four priests, three lay brothers, and ten Sacred Hearts nuns were to sail for Honolulu.

The names were announced in the monastery dining hall while forks halted halfway toward mouths and napkins slipped from laps onto the polished floor. All Damien could remember of that evening was that Pamphile's name was included on the list, and his definitely was not. He congratulated his brother and did not show his disappointment, but he must have felt it keenly. Moderation was not natural to him. His reactions were absolute, and he rarely stopped to weigh or measure. What he believed in he believed in wholly.

Stoically Damien helped Pamphile pack for the long and possibly hazardous journey across the oceans and seas. Sailing date had been set for early November, 1863, from the German port of Bremerhaven. But in September a severe epidemic of typhus broke out in Louvain and the packing was left unfinished. Priests of the city were summoned day and night to administer the last rites to dying Catholics. Pamphile trudged from household to household, rarely sleeping more than an hour and missing most meals. Streets were constantly filled with the terrible rumble of death carts. The sickness persisted, and Pamphile pushed past the limits of his fragile endurance. He contracted the rampant typhus and was forced to lie pale and feverish on his cot at the monastery.

Damien kept a worried vigil by his brother's side. Never seeming to tire, he bathed Pamphile's forehead and persuaded him to swallow warm broth from a spoon. Death hovered in the room. Writing carefully of health and sickness to his parents, Damien spoke of the "uncertainty of the morrow" and reminded Frans and Anne-Catherine that those committed to the religious life regarded themselves as "exiles" on earth, eager to enter the "true country" beyond death, the kingdom of God.

Neither parent was told of Pamphile's illness or of his amazing recovery under Damien's care. After the crisis was past, the elder brother looked nearly pencil-thin, but he was sleeping less fitfully and again eating meals. Nevertheless, he could not undertake any journey or manage a strange or strenuous mission. The small band from the Sacred Hearts would have to depart without him.

Damien was unpacking Pamphile's bags when he was struck by an intriguing idea. His brother's suitcases were empty, but they could be refilled. Pamphile was unable to travel, but Damien could take his place. And why not? What better arrangement? No one would be hurt by it. If Damien did not ask to replace Pamphile, he might not have another chance to go to the Sandwich Islands. He'd been told how seldom the congregation could afford to send priests and lay brothers to Oceania.

Impulsively Damien decided not to request permission from Father Vincke for the journey. He would write directly, and privately, to the superior general in Paris. Damien's letter, a violation of the usual rules of the order, was posted immediately upon his sealing it. He knew that his conduct was reckless, but his driving energy swept away all caution. He'd begged the superior general to let him join the mission. He'd even cleverly inserted a line about not putting the passage money to waste. Well, the deed was done. Whatever the consequences, he would pay them. He could not promise not to break rules. He could fulfill his vows of poverty and chastity, but sometimes the vow of obedience gave him trouble.

Less than a week passed after the posting of Damien's letter to Paris. Once more it was evening in the dining hall, the priests and brothers sitting in their flowing black robes buttoned from the necks to the floor-length hems. Suddenly the door was flung open, and Father Wencelas Vincke strode into the room. The superior was scowling and holding a yellow piece of parchment. Briskly he walked toward Damien, toward the impetuous young man who, four years earlier, had appeared at the monastery, a sturdy farm boy without scholarship or culture. Throughout the dining hall, Father Vincke was heard to remark, "It is rather silly of you to wish to go, Brother Damien, before you are a priest."

Damien gazed steadily into his superior's eyes. Around him was a cocoon of silence. Slowly the skin of Father Vincke's eyelids began to crinkle at the corners as, in spite of himself, he allowed a small, reluctant smile. The parchment fluttered to the table next to Damien's plate. A letter had arrived from Paris, from the superior general. The words faced upward and were brief and to the point. "For the Sandwich Islands," the letter said, "Damien de Veuster."

He was to go! He was included! He would *be* a missionary! Lifting the folds of his cassock and murmuring thanks, Damien forgot his discipline. He leaped from the table and ran to the room where Pamphile lay recovering. The usually quiet hallways echoed with his hurried, jubilant footsteps as above him, like a banner, he waved the precious letter.

Pamphile would understand his pleasure. Pamphile would celebrate his joy.

Damien's assumption was correct. Far into the morning hours, the two brothers talked in wonderment of the Sandwich Islands. When Pamphile drowsed at last and chapel bells kept caroling the passing hours, Damien slid the parchment letter under a blanket on his cot. "For the Sandwich Islands," the words said, "Damien de Veuster." Surely his dreams and his prayers to St. Xavier had been answered. And ahead of him, in the years to come, stretched a vast field for his future labors, not the fields of Tremeloo, of his youth, but an empty and fertile field for the planting, nurturing, and harvesting of the faith.

Chapter

The *R.W. Wood*, a large, three-masted vessel, was
pulled by tugboat from the wharf at Bremerhaven
and set loose in a spray of sea foam. On board was
a crew of sixteen German Protestants, sailors who
climbed the rigging like monkeys and wrestled with
giant sheets of canvas sail and webs of braided rope.
Cows and a pig were boarded off on the upper deck,
and barrels of brined pork and beef were tied down
in alleyways beside the cabins.

Damien was thrust from silence into an eddy of constant sound. In the few days before departure, he'd written his father, sent his photograph, and hiked twelve miles from Louvain to bid his mother a sad but proud farewell at the shrine of Our Lady at Montaigu. He relayed greetings from Pamphile and tearfully embraced Anne-Catherine, stumbling to express his love and gratitude for all her goodness to him.

In early November, 1863, he found himself amidst the ceaseless din made by animals, men, the ship, and the sea. Winds slammed and flattened against the sails, shouts echoed down from the spars, and hatches squealed on their hinges above the ship's cargo.

Captain Geerken was a tough-minded German, skeptical of landlubbers, but he showed a liking for Damien, perhaps because the young brother was the only Sacred Hearts traveler who did not fall seasick. Rolling from his tiny berth at dawn, Damien paced the decks with the captain in order to get his sea legs. He even clambered up the rigging with the sailors, cassock tucked up to his waist, and learned to reef a sail. If his behavior seemed unnatural for a man destined to become a priest, he did not defend it. There was work to be done on board ship. He much preferred the role of participant to passenger.

The routine of the monastery was not laid aside

during the five-month voyage to the Sandwich Islands. Hours were marked for prayer and study, and daily Mass was held in the roughest weather. Damien had been appointed sacristan and was responsible for preparing the vestments and utensils for each ceremony. He constructed a device to keep the chalice from overturning on the altar, and when supplies of wafers for the Blessed Sacrament ran out, he talked the steward into helping him experiment with batches of flour until suitable wafers were made.

On December 22, the *R.W. Wood* crossed the equator. Weeks later warm winds had given place to the chill ones of harsher latitudes. Cape Horn was sighted at the southern tip of South America, and a special Mass was said in memory of the 1843 shipwreck that plummeted one bishop, fourteen priests and lay brothers, and ten nuns to their deaths. Several days before rounding the Cape, the *R.W. Wood* was hit by a storm. Damien wrote to Pamphile of the fierce winds and voracious currents that could devour the hardiest vessel. Hatches were battened down on the ship, and the deck was forbidden to passengers. Skies blackened and waves hurled explosively over the railings, but Damien crept up to the wheel on top deck. Two helmsmen were lashed to the spokes for safety, and Captain Geerken looked like a priest himself as he huddled beside the rigging in black oilskins.

The *R.W. Wood* was in danger of sinking, as bruised as its seamen by the storm. In the cabins, the Sacred Hearts members began a *novena*, a recitation of prayers and devotions that lasted for nine consecutive days. On the ninth day, the crewmen were astonished to see the storm recede and the chill leave the air. The ship had been driven two hundred miles off course but had rounded the Horn and the danger was over. To the north lay the Pacific Ocean and another crossing of the equator.

Days were lightened by a hint of soft, tropical breeze and the glow of sun on the varnished wood of the spars. Damien and Captain Geerken resumed their morning pacing, and Damien cautiously tried his hand at converting the captain to Catholicism. But the weathered old Protestant was not about to change his ways. He regaled his companion with the story of the religious tug-of-war on the Sandwich Islands. The eight main islands in a chain of twelve had been discovered, but ignored, by Spaniards in the sixteenth century. In 1778, they were rediscovered by the Englishman James Cook, who named them the Sandwich Islands for his patron, the Earl of Sandwich.

All eight islands—Hawaii, Maui, Molokai, Lanai, Kahoolawe, Oahu, Kauai, and Niihau—were mostly populated by the Malayo-Polynesian race. In the late

1700's, they were ruled by the native king, Kamehameha I, and practiced cannibalism. By 1819, however, European religion arrived in Oceania. A French frigate anchored off the largest island, Hawaii, and a chaplain baptized two chieftains as Catholics. Then a small group of Protestant missionaries settled on the islands to compete for local converts.

Kamehameha I, explained Captain Geerken, was persuaded by the Protestants to expel the first missionary priest sent by the Catholics in 1827. Nine years later priests again tried to settle on Hawaii but were bullied and sent away. Catholics were not able to establish themselves until a second French frigate anchored off the port of Honolulu, Oahu. The frigate aimed its guns toward the town and threatened to fire unless priests were allowed to set up missions on the islands. The king relented and, by 1843, though the Catholic-Protestant rivalry continued to seethe, Hawaii, Maui, and Oahu had 12,000 Catholic converts and 100 Catholic schools.

Damien grew more anxious than ever to take part in the island mission. He'd been living on shipboard from November till March, and each morning he glanced up at the topgallant sails and prayed for a strong gust of wind from the south. On March 19, 1864, he was at the ship's railing when an emerald-hued mountain range swept up from the ocean. By afternoon, land was close enough to drop anchor. Damien watched in fascination while the waters filled with gleeful, bronze-skinned young boys who swam out in welcome from the reefs of Oahu.

With the *R.W. Wood* secured, Damien said his good-byes to Captain Geerken and the crew. Bishop Louis Maigret waited on the pier, extending a hand to the priests, lay brothers, and nuns as rowboats deposited the passengers ashore. Travel-weary but excited, they were happy to quit the close quarters of the ship. Eyes that had grown accustomed to blue water and blue sky were startled by the profusion of color in Honolulu—crimson, lime, and yellow flowers, red brick carried from England as ballast, white coral crushed on the roadways, the waxed-green surfaces of leaves. Barefoot islanders roamed the dusty streets alongside foreign sailors, and Oriental fishermen balanced poles of bleached bamboo on their shoulders.

At the cathedral, in the business district, Damien knelt by the altar. Behind him lay a journey that had separated him from all that was familiar. He'd arrived in an alien land whose customs and language he did not know, and incredibly beautiful as that land appeared it was different from any place he had ever been. Still, not everything was unfamiliar. Inside the cathedral were the universal marks of the Roman Catholic Church—the crucifix over the altar, the gilded tabernacle, the statues of the Blessed Virgin and the saints in the side chapels, with the votive candles flickering before them. These would stay the same whether in Europe or Oceania, and Damien saw them and was comforted. In scarcely more than a moment, the Honolulu cathedral had become home to him. Any Catholic church or cathedral would always be his home.

Bishop Maigret was eager for priests, and not lay brothers, to send into the fields. For the next eight weeks, Damien studied at the Sacred Hearts Fathers College at Ahumanu, Oahu, and on May 21, 1864, he was ordained a priest. He had accomplished in four years what normally required ten. The ordination was held at the cathedral in Honolulu, empowering Damien to celebrate Mass, to baptize, to confirm, to sanctify marriage, to grant absolution after confession, and to administer last rites to the dying. Slowly tracing the sign of the cross upon his chest, Damien uttered the Latin vow that rang in such splendor ever since he'd heard it as a child: *"Introibo ad altare Dei."* "I will go unto the altar of God."

Bishop Maigret assigned his new priest to the district of Puna on the island of Hawaii. Puna was without Catholic churches or schools, and Damien was the first priest to reside there in seven years. He landed from the interisland steamer and walked across the entire region, an effort that took him three days and nights. Much of the ground was of hardened lava, interrupted by deep ravines and lush, vine-covered hills. All eight islands are the tops of ancient, underwater volcanos, and in Damien's time the flowering vegetation inside the ravines and on hillsides existed nowhere else on earth. The islands were unique, a paradise of nature.

Damien traveled from village to village on Puna. He climbed and pulled himself up the hills and hacked his way through the brush, a knapsack on his back holding his breviary, a consecrated altar stone, and a few changes of clothing. Villagers invited him into their huts to share bowls of *poi*, the starchy main staple of Oceania. In two months, he had learned the Hawaiian language with its twelve consonants and five vowels. The Sacred Hearts Mission in Honolulu shipped small amounts of supplies, and he began building a church where he could preach in Hawaiian. Under a scorching sun, he was architect, builder, and carpenter, cutting down trees and sawing planks that he carried up the steep terrain by himself. The Hawaiians whispered that this priest—this stocky white man, or *haole*—could outlift any man on the island. They reported that the priest was as kind as he was strong. Affectionately they called him Kamiano, their rendering of Damien.

To Pamphile, Damien composed a long letter describing his work on Puna. "I sometimes say Mass in a native hut," he wrote, "where the Christians are accustomed to assemble on Sunday for prayer. I find sheep everywhere, but many of them are still outside the fold. Calvinism has drawn many into its net. However, the news of a priest for Puna has made them think about religion."

Damien asked Pamphile to pray for him and his "flock" so that the fire that Christ "came to cast upon the earth" would be kindled. He also implored Pamphile to send "two bells for my two new churches; they must be smaller than the one at Louvain. [And] as I have no time to write all the fathers and brothers of Louvain, please read them this letter and send a copy . . . as well to my parents."

Seven months passed in the district of Puna, and then Damien exchanged districts with another Sacred Hearts priest who was too exhausted to handle the larger area of Kohala. Having to leave his flock of parishioners was extremely painful to Damien. They had become his family, his charges, but after all he had yearned for the difficult, hadn't he? And Kohala, with its slash of precipices, its scarcity of roads or pathways, and its dangerously steep mountains, was difficult indeed.

His new charges were encamped among the mountain brambles of Kohala. Damien was issued a horse by the Sacred Hearts Mission, and he rode for weeks at a time, introducing himself to the villagers and chopping wood for a church from the mango, tamanu, and breadfruit trees. The slopes of the land were so treacherous that three pair of oxen could barely haul a cart of wooden planks to the church site. Yet whenever he had finished making the rounds of Kohala, Damien added to the structure. He also dispatched a letter to Bishop Maigret in Honolulu, asking for money to order supplies.

The money sent him was spent on paint, brushes, putty, cement, glass, kegs of nails, candles, crosses, and chalices. Damien's church was impressive, with its cross raised over the door, but no sooner was it finished than he mailed off requests for more money and supplies. "You're pestering me," Bishop Maigret replied in good humor. "You are of fine service to the Mission, but you must learn to be patient."

Damien would never really learn how to be patient. His energy precluded patience. Each year of his eight years in Kohala, he managed to build another church. If he was not building or preaching, he planted crops on the flank of a hill for a harvest of potatoes and kidney beans. His hands were constantly blistered by axe, spade, or hammer. Squeezing a pen between stiffened fingers, he wrote to his family, to Pamphile, and to Father Vincke. Confiding in Pamphile that bouts of melancholy sometimes seized him, he assured his brother that he distracted himself by scything a path through dense bushes or fashioning benches for Sunday service. "Let us be in the hands of God," he said in a letter, "as tools in the hands of a skillful workman."

A distant village in Kohala had never been visited by any priest. In spite of warnings, Damien strapped on his knapsack and set out by horse for it. Two days into the jungle, he had to leave the overheated animal with a local family. Alone, he swam across a shark-infested, inland sea and climbed mountains by grabbing onto vines and rocks. Crossing a network of vegetation, he slipped and dug his fingers into the soil to save himself from plunging to a violent death.

On the fourth day, Damien scaled a mountaintop. His cassock was in shreds, and his boots were peeling off his feet. Cuts and bruises marked his body and three fingernails had been ripped out, but he crawled from rock to rock to make the descent. He was only yards from his destination when fatigue overcame him, and he tumbled onto his head and lost consciousness. At sunrise, he was discovered by a villager, who washed and revived him. He walked then among the cluster of mountain huts and smiled at the welcoming people. He would not speak of his injuries or of his struggles on the mountains. There was a dying child to be baptized, a Mass to be performed, a couple to be married.

On other occasions, Damien had to deal with danger from the Kohala people themselves. Not everyone in the district looked with favor on the priest from the Sacred Hearts. He was *haole*, a white man, and white sailors were the ones who'd brought tuberculosis, syphilis, and leprosy to the islands. Many of the inhabitants had their own form of worship and scoffed at the teachings of Jesus Christ. Cult leaders exercised their power and reclaimed some of Damien's converts. There were rumors of bloody animal sacrifice in the hills and of mysterious rites performed by a newly initiated cult.

One evening, when Damien sat reading in his grass hut, he heard the sound of drums and a piercing, inhuman scream. In the ferns outside the hut was lodged a crude stone idol that leaned above a rock stained with fresh clots of blood. Disgusted, Damien knocked over the idol and used it to smash the rock into scattered pieces. He snapped two branches from a tree and tied them with vines into a cross, pushing the bottom tip into the ground. Surveying the scene, he lifted his mudstained clerical hat off his head and arranged it carefully beneath the cross.

Damien's silent message must have been seen. Soon there was a shell filled with dark and foul-smelling ashes roped to the door of his hut. Aware that he musn't lose face with his converts, Damien tied the shell to the tail of a rooting hog and let the animal romp through the village. That night the hog, disembowled, was spread at his door and a shrill staccato drumming started up in the darkness.

Damien was angry. He was not certain of how Father Vincke might have counseled him to act, but he could not respond meekly. He could only hope that he was not a disappointment to his church. A woman pulled at his sleeve, whispering of a frightful ceremony in the hills, and he marched off into the night toward the drumming. He was on the trails and rock-strewn paths for an hour before he saw a suffused glare of red light. From deep inside a cave came the muffled scream of someone or something in torture.

Damien strode into the cave and was confronted by a semicircle of twenty or thirty men crouched beneath four flaming torches. Beside them was a heap of glistening bones, the cracked skulls, skeletons, and limbs of slaughtered animals. Moisture oozed on the slimy walls, and a smell of bitter herbs steamed from a vat. Suddenly Damien faced a naked figure who tore open the throat of a butchered dog. Blood spurted into a gourd, and the dog was tossed onto the pile of bones.

The wizened leader came slowly forward to the

half circle of men, bearing a dagger and a wooden puppet. Damien peered closer. He recognized the squat likeness, face and hands smeared with white paint and body clothed in a miniature cassock. The wooden doll was an effigy of himself. A tiny cross hung at the neck, and a string of rosary beads—ones that Damien had missed from his own hut—were twisted at the waist. The dagger was slowly poised over the puppet's chest.

Enraged now, Damien burst into the crescent of men and watched them rear back. Taking advantage of the moment, he snatched the puppet from the ringleader and hurled it to the dirt floor. He would prove the sorcery a lie. He smashed the puppet's body with his boot, making its rosary beads spin away like toy balls. The wooden figure crunched sharply under Damien's heel, and he saw the horrified expressions of the onlookers. He was supposed to be struck down apparently by the retribution of Evil Powers. Instead, he straightened up and frowned at the startled men. Their leader squatted in a corner, muttering to himself.

Unfastening a torch from its post, Damien swung it back and forth. "Go home," he told the men. "I have seen you in the villages. You have wives and children. They would not want you believing in this ugly and foolish witchcraft. The air here is unhealthy. Go home to your families."

Sheepishly the men disbanded their circle and slipped off into the night. Damien blew out the torches and prepared for another hour's walk across the twisted trails to his grass hut. His neck was taut and his face felt flushed, but he was free of his uncertainty. If he'd lost control of his temper, if his crushing of the puppet had even given him a bit of pleasure, he'd made his point in the dark mouth of that hillside cave. The powers of evil, with their effigies and sorcery, their witch doctors and black magic, had truly been no match for the powers of good.

Chapter

In Honolulu, the *Nuhou*, a newspaper, printed stories of world events, but news traveled slowly across the seas. The islands were located over two thousand miles from the west coast of America, and a month could pass in the transit of mail. Letters came to Damien from Pamphile and from Tremeloo, but he saw himself cut off from life beyond the islands. He had written his sister Pauline before learning that she'd died in her convent in 1872. He had read late reports of the Franco-Prussian War just as word arrived that French troops were defeated at Sedan.

Building supplies were shipped to the Sandwich Islands from Europe and America in return for sugarcane grown by the islanders. Sailors brought toys and trinkets to win the favors of local women and told glorious tales of England, France, Germany, China, India, and the Americas. What they also brought, however, was disease to the island people. No matter how slow the journey of ships, no matter how estranged the outside world, disease claimed passage along with the toys, trinkets, and supplies.

The most hideous of the imported diseases was leprosy, the "death before death" of the ancient Egyptians. Beginning with nerve pains or itching spots on the skin, leprosy was a chronic and fatal infection that degenerated the tissues of the body, organs, and nervous system into a ghastly array of open sores and rotten flesh. Advanced leprosy, progressing for as long as fifteen years, caused swelling, nodules, and tumors, muscle impairment, loss of nerve sensation, and the destruction of mucous membranes in the respiratory tract and eyes. The disease was gruesomely disfiguring. Lepers in the Bible's

Book of Leviticus were banished for being "unclean," and the disease could be traced back to 2000 B.C. in India and China and to 1500 B.C. in Japan. The true origin of leprosy is debated by physicians and historians. It may have spawned on the moist and marshy banks of Egypt's Nile River or in the exotic and mysterious Orient, then been carried by the wars of Darius, Alexander the Great, and the Romans to Western countries. Eventually it invaded Oceania.

Outside Damien's churches in Kohala, he'd stopped to offer special solace to lepers who sneaked onto the grounds to listen to snatches of choir music through an open window or door. He'd noticed that the number of lepers had increased, the smiling, broad-faced islanders deformed into bloated creatures whose flesh reeked with an overpowering odor. Reddish-brown eruptions assailed the face, ears, and limbs, turning the skin rough and scaly. Eyes reddened, eyebrows fell out, lips were engorged, and the earlobes swelled from infection until they distended into huge masses that hung to the shoulders. Decades would pass before medical science discovered the enormous quantities of bacilli multiplying in a leprous person. Damien saw only the outward evidence of decay, the burst of crusted growths on reddened skin into pus-filled or gangrenous sores, the disintegration of bone so that nose, fingers, and toes sagged inward against the flesh.

In 1850, a Board of Health had been established in Honolulu, and the *Nuhou* printed editorials about the dreadful rise of leprosy. By 1865, the year after Damien landed at Puna, the reigning king was stampeded into action by the newspaper stories. He instructed the Board of Health to select a place for isolating lepers in order to protect the remainder of the population. The site chosen was a small northern promontory on the island of Molokai, a ten-square-mile strip of land that formed a natural prison because the shoreline was edged with cliffs and the promontory was separated from the island proper by a 1500-foot tower of rock, the *pali.*

Damien had never visited Molokai. He'd heard that it was thinly populated, strewn with mammoth rocks, and slashed by jutting precipices. The lepers in his district and on the other islands had largely ignored Board of Health orders to report for diagnosis and exile to Molokai's tiny settlement of Kalawao in the set-aside area. Families were extremely loving, and they balked at having their lepers taken from them. Despite the risk of infection, a leper's relatives often deserted the villages and hid in the hills with a sick or dying man, woman, or child.

One Kohala husband barricaded himself and his

leper wife behind a fortress of rocks on a craggy mountain slope. The police, who had stepped up their efforts to segregate lepers, tried to corral the diseased wife onto a steamer sailing for Molokai. The husband, however, armed himself with a shotgun and defiantly fired it down the mountain. Damien did not want any lives lost, and he pushed past the uniformed authorities. Unprotected, he climbed a rugged little mountain pathway and shouted, "Don't shoot. Do not fire. It is your friend, Kamiano."

The husband warily kept his aim, but Damien stood for hours beneath the bulwark of rocks. Hoarsely he explained that segregation was necessary to stop leprosy from infecting the villages. The husband shouted back that he merely wished to keep his wife to himself, to care for her until she died, but Damien answered that the woman might die much too soon if she resisted arrest and were shot by police. At sunset, a weary and gravel-voiced Damien was followed down the mountain by the man and his wife. The couple had been promised that the police would do nothing in reprisal and that the husband could chance disease and death on Molokai with his wife and other lepers.

Only toward the end of his eight years in Kohala did Damien learn the truth about Kalawao settlement on Molokai. The Board of Health had concealed the state of sanitation, food, and lodging. They'd assumed that, given seeds and tools, the lepers would till the land, plant crops, and become self-sufficient enough not to create a disturbance. They were going to die anyway, the Board members said. It would be best for them to be left quite alone. The sight or smell of their rotting limbs and distorted flesh was too gruesome for the sensibilities of healthy people.

The lepers had not met the expectations of the Board of Health. Wrested from their families, herded aboard the grimy, interisland steamer, the *Kilauea*, and abandoned on the shore at Molokai, they were angry and depressed. At Kalawao, they found dilapidated huts and a barnlike "hospital" in which they were supposed to grovel on filthy grass mats and await the mercy of death. No houses, stores, roads, doctors, nurses, ministers, or priests existed on the promontory. The wind howled across the sheer walls of rock, the beastly sickness claimed parts of the body, and the lepers had no interest in planting crops for a tomorrow that could bring nothing but worsening illness and a lonely death.

From the roots of the *ti* plant, a bitter alcohol was brewed that kept the several hundred lepers in a state of constant intoxication. Card playing and prostitution were the entertainment, and the farm tools provided by the Board of Health rusted on the windswept ground. Forced to sustain the lepers, the Board periodically sent casks of salt beef, cured salmon, and *poi* on the steamer. The *Kilauea's* crewmen refused to approach Molokai's pier and threw the supplies toward swimming lepers in the swirling waters. A few bellowing cows were shoved overboard, and any newly condemned victims might be dropped from the steamer railing to swim or to drown.

Since there was no cure for leprosy, the Board of Health rarely shipped any medication. Remedies had been tried to relieve the agony of lepers, but none were more than briefly soothing. Moses had advised oil or tree sap for leprosy, and Louis XI of France—who'd mistakenly believed he was a leper—bathed himself in turtles' blood. In some countries, the venom of poisonous snakes was scrubbed on leprous sores or the ill person was undressed and encased by the carcass of a disemboweled ox. Physicians in Europe, Asia, and the United States had, at various times, prescribed swallowing iodine, doses of arsenic and strychnine, or salicylic acid with arsenite of potash. Suggested skin applications included gurjun oil from the Andaman Islands, a lotion of corrosive sublimate, beeswax, lard, cod-liver oil, gold leaf, copper, lead, or a pasty mixture of dog manure and molasses. In Oceania, these remedies were called *haole* magic that failed; the witch doctors preferred mountain apple, turmeric, and wild ginger, which also failed.

Occasionally one of the twenty-one priests on the Sandwich Islands had visited Kalawao settlement, returning after several days in silent horror. A Brother Bertrand stayed just long enough to erect a small church, named after St. Philomena, but the Catholic lepers had forsaken religion. Drunkenness and despair erased all vestiges of decency. Lepers staggered past the sicker residents of the settlement, those who could no longer drag themselves over the ground, without heeding their pitiful pleas for water. Other lepers, on the brink of death, were buried while they moaned or screamed in pain. Wrapped in a moldy blanket, they were dumped from a wheelbarrow into a deep ravine or laid in a grave so shallow that wild hogs came to feast upon rag-covered flesh.

Damien was told of Molokai's lepers by some of his fellow priests. After his own confession had been heard by Father Ropert or Father Clément, he sat in one of the churches he'd built at Kohala and heard the grim, ghastly stories of Molokai. The lepers, he was informed, were treated like monsters and, therefore, were making monsters of themselves. Killings occurred on Molokai, but the police who had been dispatched to restore order found the lepers using a weapon more powerful than loaded guns. Hooting, the outcasts rushed to embrace the policemen, rubbing them with raw, ulcerous wounds. Repelled and gagging, the officers fled from Kalawao to rowboats beneath the outer ring of cliffs.

The lepers, like a band of grotesque but gleeful soldiers, rushed behind to the narrow shoreline. In crackling unison, they shouted out, " '*A'ole kānāwai ma keia wahi*!" "Here there is no law!"

Damien had listened carefully to the stories of Kalawao settlement. If there was no law among the wretched lepers, or no compassion at the Board of Health, what about a higher law, a law of Divine Origin, God, of Love, of the moral principles of Christ? Vigorously Damien continued his work at Kohala, but thoughts of the lepers lingered in his mind. Almost every week he saw another leper taken weeping and desolate from the arms of family and friends. If only the afflicted could be sent to a community of comfort and care, of worthwhile occupation. But instead they were sent to Molokai, to Kalawao, to a monstruous Hell upon earth.

In the spring of 1873, a new king, Lunalilo, had risen to power in the Sandwich Islands. Newspapers

58

urged the king to visit Kalawao and to see for himself if the horror stories were true. But King Lunalilo was afraid of leprosy. He would not consent to go to Molokai and instead released a brief message of condolence for the lepers. That May, from the island of Maui, Bishop Maigret called upon six Sacred Hearts priests of the Mission to help consecrate a large church at Wailuku. Damien was among the priests called, and he went at once by interisland steamer to join his bishop.

After the consecration, Bishop Maigret suggested that the priests discuss Kalawao settlement. Something must be done, the bishop said. The Sacred Hearts Mission had, in a sense, watched Molokai from afar. The superiors had balked at assigning a permanent priest to the lepers since the assignment could mean an irredeemable sentence of death.

Shaking his head, Bishop Maigret told the priests that Kalawao was now populated with seven hundred lepers. History showed that the disease had sudden rises and falls in numbers of victims. Poor sanitation might have caused some of the outbreaks, but during the twelfth and thirteenth centuries a quarter of Europe's people had been attacked by leprosy. The Church had tried to befriend the ill, lodging them in "lazar houses," named for Lazarus, the leprous beggar of the Bible. Yet many thousands were treated as loathsome objects. Did the priests know, asked Bishop Maigret, that medieval Europe had declared lepers legally dead, banishing them into the wilderness to carry rattles that warned passersby of their approach?

Yes, Damien answered, he had studied the subject in Louvain. St. Xavier, to whom he'd often prayed, was the one who had protected lepers. Damien had read the instructions for lepers of the Middle Ages, those driven in terror from cities and towns. They were to wear gloves and touch nothing with their bare hands. They were not to enter churches, mills, bakeries, or markets. They were outcasts and must dwell alone. They were not to answer when spoken to until the speaker was safely to the windward of any leper. And in Marseilles or Edinburgh, if the rules were flouted, a leper might be hung, burned, or driven nude into the fields.

Kalawao settlement, the Bishop said softly, was being called Ka Lua Kupapa'u, corpse pit or tomb. Did the priests have suggestions of their own for the good of the Mission? Yes, Damien answered again. With the other five priests, he devised a plan to rotate assignment among the lepers. Each priest would volunteer his services and stay for a specified length of time. The plan was gladly received by Bishop Maigret. Not to have to condemn anyone permanently to Molokai would be a blessing. But who would be the first priest to volunteer?

Damien leaped forward. "I want to go!" he said, as recklessly as he once had written from Louvain to his superior general in Paris. "A newly ordained priest can be assigned my post at Kohala. He will be welcome there."

Bishop Maigret slowly nodded. "I never would have placed this hardship on you, Father Damien," the bishop said, "but if you are so eager, I respectfully accept your offer."

Damien requested permission to leave that very evening for Molokai. He was concerned that the Board of Health, which favored Protestant clergymen, might try to delay him. He persuaded Bishop Maigret to let him board the *Kilauea*, which was just loading at the wharf at Wailuku. However, the bishop insisted on accompanying Damien from Maui to the shores of Molokai.

The date was May 10, 1873. By coincidence, perhaps, Damien de Veuster was thirty-three years old, the age of Christ at the crucifixion, a coincidence of which he was certainly aware. He stood on the *Kilauea*'s deck with his breviary pressed against his chest. So determined had he been to sail for Molokai, to tackle the place where there was "no law," that he'd gone without packing his few belongings or saying good-bye at Kohala to his latest flock of beloved "children." Surrounding him were nearly fifty lepers in various stages of decay, and a fly-infested cargo of mangy cattle. Several of the lepers cast flower necklaces, or *leis*, into Maui's waters, signifying a hope to sail home someday, but the hope was futile.

No one could know Damien's thoughts as he walked among the despairing lepers. The *Kilauea* lurched beneath him; his cassock flapped about his legs. He might have been remembering the sacred book *The Imitation of Christ*. He might have contemplated the likelihood that, by volunteering to live at Kalawao settlement, he was choosing a supreme mortification of the flesh. Having told Pamphile that he and all others were "exiles" on earth, he had elected to become an even more extreme exile, to make himself an outcast among outcasts. He must have had some inkling that he was taking a great step, for Damien later remarked that after he'd left Kohala for Wailuku to see his bishop, he felt an overwhelming presentiment that he would never return. And except for a month or less at a time, Damien's descent into the corpse tomb of lepers became the permanent mode and measure of his life.

Chapter **5**

"To begin is nothing," Damien once wrote Father Vincke. "The hard thing is to persevere." During his first weeks on Molokai, Damien slept under a giant pandanus tree. He had little time to set up lodging, and he usually did not sleep until after midnight, his mind too benumbed by the day to notice the mynah birds and sparrows rustling above him or the centipedes, tree rats, scorpions, and roaches that scurried over the ground. Dark lava cliffs closeted Kalawao settlement with all its misery, and not even a magenta dawn could dispel the living nightmare.

Lepers at Kalawao were in far worse condition than Damien had imagined. An English priest who'd visited the settlement had come to the cathedral in Honolulu, sobbing uncontrollably. The reasons were now clear. Some of Molokai's lepers seemed to have no faces. Craters of pus leaked where eyes had once been, and ulcerated holes took the place of absent noses and mouths. Bodies were distended while arms and legs might be reduced to ragged stumps. One of the lepers sat watching Damien's arrival from the front of a soggy grass hut. Mutely he cut off a rotting finger, its nerves anesthetized by the disease, and threw the severed flesh over his shoulder like a piece of garbage.

Observed by the lepers, Damien investigated every corner of Kalawao settlement. Rains had drenched the soil and left a splattering of mud over the skimpy lean-tos and huts. A few inhabitants sneered at Damien when he landed, but three dwarflike young girls stumbled toward him with wet orange blossoms and yellow hibiscus. He took the muddy flowers from their hands and bent down to thank them. The girls were badly infected, exiled on Molokai without parents and shunned by the healthy children who'd been born to leper women in the colony without contracting the sickness. Damien walked with the girls from Kalaupapa, the landing area on the shore. At the small, unused church of St. Philomena, he stepped gratefully into a dark interior. Dust and dirt caked the narrow benches, and Damien asked the children to bring him thick tree branches and reeds. Improvising a broom, he spent four hours of his first day on Molokai sweeping out the church and cleaning the altar.

On his third morning, Damien considered the chaos of the settlement and began deciding what he should do. The challenge and burden of Molokai would have terrified most men. Had help appeared from a corps of doctors, engineers, and construction workers, still the task of putting the colony in order might have seemed overwhelming. But Damien viewed the barren land, the shambles of huts, the filthy "hospital" building, the ghastly, gangrenous wounds of the lepers and envisioned how everything could change. Writing to Bishop Maigret, he made application to remain permanently on Molokai. "It is absolutely necessary," he said with utter conviction, as if he'd always believed it. He requested also a box of devotional books, altar breads, rosaries, shirts, trousers, shoes, and a clock. The box was dispatched by boat, but the decision to allow him to stay among the lepers and not rotate the assignment was slower to arrive.

Bishop Maigret wrote to the superior general in Paris, informing him that at Damien's departure several Honolulu newspapers pounced on the priest as a triumphant answer to the problem of Kalawao settlement. The publicity had evoked over a hundred dollars in contributions for Father Damien "and his lepers," and even the Protestant press called Damien a "Christian hero." What must be said? asked Bishop Maigret. Plans were for Damien to be a temporary priest on Molokai, but with his determination and the good effect on the public, perhaps Divine Providence had spoken. Should he be permitted his request? In a month, word reached the bishop from Paris: Father Damien could remain at his post.

And so, as Damien wrote to Pamphile, he would be "a leper among the lepers." With wood sent from the Sacred Hearts Mission, he built a small presbytery, a mere sixteen-by-ten-foot hut, and equipped it with a sleeping mat and a tiny kerosene stove for boiling water. A leprous doctor, banished to the settlement but unable to function, taught him how to sterilize knives and scissors, to wash and bandage sores, and to amputate gangrenous limbs. He arose each morning before the sun was visible on the cliffs and went to kneel by the altar of St. Philomena. Then he set out to visit all the lepers at Kalawao and those who lived by the shore at Kalaupapa. His visits involved four entire days of every week. On Sundays, he held Mass and Vespers, lifting the sickest lepers onto the benches of the church.

Instinctively Damien knew that he could not bring permanent change to Kalawao settlement without removing a barrier—the ancient repulsion at *touching* a leper's body. If he were to reach the spirits of these hideously ill human beings, he must be willing to touch them, embrace them, anoint them with salves or oils to soothe their wounds and bestow the last rites for a blessed death. In the filthy lean-tos, he shared their meals, squatting on the ground and eating from bowls of *poi*. He puffed on a pipe that he'd begun carrying with him and invited groups of the men to inhale from the pipe in turn. "I am Kamiano," he told them. "I will not abandon you."

He was, of course, courting disaster—foolishly, his critics said—but safety was not in his mission. What he braved in those torrid huts is almost beyond comprehension. To confront the living death suffered by lepers and not sink into gloom required a constant renewal of faith. To be nearly overcome by the stench of rotting flesh and not dissolve in horror drew on all the self-control he possessed. Damien's lighted pipe helped mask the insufferable odors, but for months he was beset by headaches and nausea. He'd been compelled, he wrote in a letter, to "run outside the huts to breathe fresh air," yet he buoyantly resumed his duties. He cleaned and dressed wounds as if he were handling delicate flowers. Biscuits, candies, and rosaries, sent from well-wishers in Honolulu, were pulled from his pockets and passed about to the ill.

In time, Damien's nausea and headaches disappeared, and if he felt occasional flashes of a melancholy that he'd once confided to Pamphile, he still learned to love the lepers as he had loved his flocks at Puna and Kohala. The body, he said, his own as well as anyone's, would rot quickly enough anyhow. The soul alone was what counted.

Water used for drinking and bathing sores at Kalawao settlement had to be transported in rusty cans from a hidden gulch. Many of the crippled lepers had died not of their disease but of thirst. Instead of writing to Bishop Maigret, Damien wrote directly to the Board of Health. Wood should be sent, he said, for building decent cottages, as should clothing, medical supplies, more food, pipes to carry water, and a *real* doctor for Heaven's sake! The requests were filed away unanswered, but Damien did not keep quiet. He might be isolated among the lepers, but his voice and his determination reached Honolulu. Letter after letter bombarded the offices of the Board of Health. The *Nuhou* reporters unearthed Damien's complaints and publicized the stinginess of the Board's food supplies and their meager allowance of six dollars per year per leper.

The pressure of the editorials and the somehow looming figure of "this meddlesome priest, Father Damien" made the Board of Health finally send a cargo of tools and metal pipes. At the edge of a valley called Waihanau, Damien tracked down a tropical pool that was wide enough and deep enough not to dry out, and he walked from hut to hut at Kalawao tempting a few of the more able-bodied lepers to help him. In the sand at the shoreline, he sketched a rough blueprint to show how the pipes might be laid from pool to village, and then he and his helpers spent taxing days hauling and fitting the pipes. Spigots were installed near each of the huts, and dozens of lepers limped out to feel the miracle of cool, precious water bubbling over blemished limbs.

The day after the pipes were laid Damien was felling trees with an axe and sawing them into planks. He was going to enclose the makeshift graveyard with a protective picket fence, and he worked amidst decomposing flesh in open graves and sun-bleached bones scattered by ravenous hogs. The graveyard was an acknowledged center at Kalawao settlement. Every day brought death to one or more of the lepers, and dying itself was not mourned by the ill. The fence completed, Damien began digging deeper graves and constructing coffins. Pamphile wrote from Louvain that he was studying for a doctorate in theology. Little did the elder brother know, as he pored over books in a clean room at a clean desk, that Damien was knee-deep in a muddy, putrefied graveyard, cassock stained and hat tied on by two strings, nailing together what would eventually amount to over two thousand coffins.

Water pipes and Damien's coffins, however, did not mollify the more debauched of the lepers. Drunken orgies and prostitution continued. Bruises and blood from fistfights mixed with the rupturing clusters of leprous sores. The lives of the lepers were doomed, and many cared only for dulling their misery and indulging their whims. They spat at Damien if he approached and rushed at him to rub their pus on his arms. Yet he did not flinch under the touch of the untouchables. The drinking and prostitution must stop, he told them. He was not frightened by their illness. He would not tolerate them behaving as beasts. If he heard the wild laughter that suggested an orgy, he marched into the midst of any group, no matter what was going on, knocked over cans of liquor with the stick that he brandished, shooed the male lepers away from the females, and thundered in ferocious Hawaiian at the troublemakers. He captured their respect, if not their conversion to Catholicism. He would have things *his* way, a way that was changing disorder to order. He would draw them into his circle, as he'd once drawn in and tended the sheep in Tremeloo.

In the summer after he received permission to stay on Molokai, Damien was beckoned from his presbytery by a shriveled old woman, her face distorted by tumors. The woman was not Catholic, she said. She had never attended Mass at St. Philomena's or joined the lepers who were baptized into Damien's faith. But her son was in death throes— his open sores had scabbed over in the mark of death—and he was a good Catholic convert and pleading for the priest. Would Damien come? Would he follow the woman to her hut?

In a hovel of dried branches and reeds, Damien bent over a heap of mildewed clothes on a mat of rushes. Somewhere inside the heap was a human form, the hands bloated and fingerless, the head devoid of normal ears. Smothering with the terrible odor in the air, Damien staggered outside until he

71

could stand more firmly on his feet. When once more he bent beside the mat, he saw that the dying man hugged a blood-spattered prayer book. In a guttural, rasping whisper, the leper begged for the last rites of the Church, the sacrament of extreme unction administered by a priest through prayers and the anointing of the eyes, nose, and feet with oil.

Damien dipped his fingers into a bottle of holy oil that he'd brought from the presbytery. St. Augustine had described a sacrament as the "visible form of an invisible grace," and Damien's lips moved in prayer as he touched the tattered ear tissue and the black-encrusted residue of nose. But as he turned toward the leper's feet, Damien was stunned. One foot looked to be in constant motion, though the leper was so weak that he could not stir.

Again Damien bent down and nearly fainted, for the skin of the leper's foot was split open and inside a gaping cavity were clusters of slimy gray maggots, squirming as they fed on rotten flesh.

Fighting down the need to vomit, Damien prayed over the dying man. Maggots were of the earth, not of the spirit. The leper's mother squatted nearby, observing Damien and her son. At the moment of death, a half sigh of contentment escaped from the leper and the prayer book slipped from his grasp.

72

The old woman tapped Damien's shoulder. Her son had died unafraid, she whispered. Damien's faith must have a magic. Could she be received into the Church? Might she be baptized? Damien nodded his welcome and covered the body on the mat with a torn sack. That day two souls had been enfolded by the message of Christ—the soul just departed from its earthly body and the one still embodied, a living testament to God.

As the need for more supplies for Kalawao weighed on Damien more heavily, he decided to appear in person at the Board of Health. A storm had destroyed most of the colony's huts, and if enough wood were requisitioned by the Board, Damien could build cottages. Honolulu was not far and a schooner had anchored off Molokai, so he rowed out to it. That afternoon he knocked on the door of the offices to which he'd sent so many letters of request and complaint.

The reception given Damien at the Board of Health was icy. The meddlesome peasant priest, the recipient of praise and publicity that cast an unfavorable light on the Board for its treatment of lepers, had dared showed up without courtesy of an appointment. He was constrained to wait in a stuffy room for hours. He was repeatedly instructed to state both his name and the nature of his business.

When he was admitted to the Board president, a man with a smirk and a well-fed, protruding stomach, Damien lost his temper.

Gesturing and pacing the floor, he berated the Board for its negligence and for the desperate plight of the lepers. The Board must take action, Damien said. How would the president enjoy suffering an illness with no doctor to attend him, no medicines to soothe his sores, no clean change of clothes or bedding, no decent food or house to harbor him? Haughtily the president replied that Damien was not an administrator. The priest was a man of religion who should learn to perform his duties and *nothing more*. Why, the president asked, had Damien left the settlement? Hadn't he volunteered to stay? Didn't the royal law forbid anyone at Kalawao from interacting with healthy citizens?

Abruptly the Board president waved Damien away. Other appointments were scheduled, he said, and he could not listen further. If Damien chose to return to Molokai, he would be isolated there. He must not leave, nor could he have visitors. In fact, all ship captains would be advised that no one from the settlement might take passage and that only lepers were to land at Kalaupapa. If Damien disobeyed the law, he would be arrested and jailed like a common criminal.

From Molokai, Damien wrote another of his letters to the members of the Board of Health. He would not accept their nonsense, he said. On occasion, he had to see his bishop, and the lepers needed a spokesman. If he judged that a trip from the settlement was necessary, he would travel whenever and wherever he must, no matter how unfairly he was treated.

Damien was called "obstinate," "officious," and "headstrong" by the Board of Health. He was always to be at odds with them. The more haunted he felt by the lepers' suffering, the more he railed at the pomposity and neglect of government officials. The Board members went home at night to comfortable homes. They slept on feathered mattresses and ate from crystal plates. They had not sailed into the hell of the corpse tomb and would have run screaming from the lepers. Let them be safe then at a distance. But where was their compassion? Where were their hearts?

Months later, when Bishop Maigret traveled on the *Kilauea*, hoping to hear confession and give absolution to Damien, he was reminded by the captain that he could not disembark at Molokai. The *Kilauea* dropped anchor while the bishop pleaded his case against such rigidity, but the captain kept reciting the newest law. On shore, Damien saw the argument and jumped into an old rowboat at Kalau-papa. With churning oars, he rowed out to the steamer, his excitement mounting as he neared his bishop. He would ask to come aboard just for confession. Surely the captain knew the importance to a Catholic of confession of sins, of the sacrament of penance.

Leeward of the *Kilauea*, Damein was flatly refused access to the deck. The law forbade it, he was told. Could anyone have answered, " *'A'ole kānāwai ma keia wahi*" ("In this place there is no law")? Bishop Maigret gazed wistfully down at Damien. Less than fifty feet separated the two men, yet they had none of the privacy required for confession. Damien sat on a wooden plank in the rowboat and stared up at the steamer. He had always found a way to do what he most desired, what he thought was right, even if that way were "obstinate" and "headstrong." And now, there on the water, he wished to make his confession to his bishop. He yearned to begin the age-old invocation, "Pray, Father, bless me, for I have sinned."

Calling to Bishop Maigret, Damien suddenly announced that he would make confession at that moment by the side of the steamer. Unashamed, in full earshot of the curious crewmen, he ignored their casual jokes and fell to his knees in the rowboat.

A pulse of waves rocked him from side to side, but his voice did not quaver as he started the details of his confession.

Absolution was granted by a tearful Bishop Maigret. The non-Catholic crew, their jokes silenced, sensed that Damien had performed an act of emotional bravery. Rising from his knees, Damien nodded to his bishop and sat down on the dampened plank. He gripped the oars of the boat, and, his back rigidly straight under his black cassock, he rowed in the direction of Kalaupapa. Sweeping through the foam and flash of the waves, Damien cut a path toward the island of Molokai. Waiting for him at their prison were "his poor sick children," his "outcasts sentenced by the rest of men" as he'd come to call them to Pamphile.

Not once did Damien glance up across the heaving sea at the *Kilauea* still riding at anchor.

Chapter 6

To the south of the narrow promontory that contained Kalawao settlement, separated from the lepers by the awesome cliffs of the *pali*, were the healthy inhabitants of Molokai. Protestant missions had been active there, and Damien, in spite of the enormity of his burdens at Kalawao, felt concerned about the Catholic converts in the south. The Government had forbidden him to visit anyone outside the settlement, but his obstinacy grew stronger.

The Board of Health had appointed a superintendent named Meyer to keep watch on the colony and submit monthly reports from the safe distance of southern Molokai. A German Protestant, R. W. Meyer nevertheless seemed to wield little influence over members of the Board. Frequently Damien asked Meyer to write to Honolulu for supplies, but if none were sent he took to pen and ink himself.

On a cool autumn night in 1874, strapping his portable altar over his shoulders, he climbed a trail up the *pali*. He'd seen cows and goats, imported by Europeans to Oceania, lose their bearings on the cliffs and tumble thousands of feet to a thundering death. Every twist or turn of the trail had its dangers —jagged crevices or tunnels in the brittle lava, rocks that could come hurtling down against one's body and cause a disastrous fall. Damien had tied his cassock around his waist and borrowed a pair of pants from a leper who helped him officiate at Mass. Defiantly he made his journey over the *pali* to visit the Catholic parishioners on the other side of the island. Only the moonlight guided him between frozen hollows of lava, and he climbed as he had climbed at Kohala, fingers bleeding from thistles and boots punctured by the scrape of stone. The hardiest Hawaiians required an hour and a half to reach the crest of the primeval cliffs. Damien made the same journey in forty-five minutes.

At the foot of the trail on the other side, he asked a family for directions to the cabin of Superintendent Meyer in the district of Kalae. The superintendent was shocked to see Damien. Meyer should have had the priest arrested by authorities for breaking regulations, but he could not help sympathizing with Damien's motives. As before, he was impressed by this man of the cloth who did not fit the stock image of a priest. There was nothing meek or mild about him, no pristine white collar at the neck, no carefully manicured nails. He was neither a scholarly nor ethereal man. Father Damien of the lepers was splotched with dirt, bleeding at the hands, dressed in a strange costume of striped pants and faded, rope-tied cassock, and he was grinning his feisty grin and asking Meyer if he could borrow a horse to ride among the Catholic converts.

The last time he'd lent Damien a horse, Meyer replied—before the Government ban—it was returned drenched with sweat and frothing from overwork. Ah, *that* horse, Damien countered. That grand animal toiled in service to the Mission and to the lepers. What better productivity for animal or man?

Sighing in resignation, Meyer excused himself to fetch a horse from the barn. Somehow Damien could not be stymied. The priest had the simplicity and earnestness of a child. Yet, as Meyer knew first-hand, he was as capable of a wily temper tantrum as he was of the generous, persuasive, and heroic gesture.

In Damien's rare moments of leisure at Kalawao, he strolled through the graveyard, built small gifts of furniture for the lepers, or wrote letters to Louvain, Paris, and Tremeloo. At night, the skin on his legs had been stinging him, but it was relieved by applications of grease. Otherwise, he was as energetic as ever. If a steamer delivered better rations of food that he'd bullied out of the Board of Health or deposited a huddled caravan of lepers, Damien was at the shoreline in greeting. He fed the frightened newcomers and kept them at the presbytery until he arranged lodging. "I am still enjoying perfect health," he'd written his mother on December 8, 1874. "My dinner consists of rice, meat, coffee, and a few biscuits. For supper, I take what was left at dinner, with a cup of tea, the water for which I boil over a lamp. . . . You see, I live very well; I don't starve. I am not much at home in the daytime. After dark, I say my breviary by the light of the lamp, I study a bit, or write a letter. So don't wonder at getting only one letter a year from me. . . . I have been obliged to steal an hour or two from my sleep now, in order to write this letter and some others which I must send to Europe. The new year is at hand: I wish you all a very happy one. Don't forget me in your daily prayers. Joseph Damien de Veuster."

The return news from Tremeloo advised Damien that his father, Frans, had died but that his mother included her distant son in all her prayers. Sadly Damien lit an altar candle in memory of his father. He had known that he might never again see his family. His parents, brothers, and sisters had been separated from him by the distance in miles and years; his nieces and nephews were strangers to him. He'd prodded Pamphile to petition assignment to the Sandwich Islands, but such an event did not occur.

Another letter from Europe, however, occasioned celebration at Kalawao. It also arrived in 1874 with a message that announced a breakthrough in research on leprosy. A doctor from Norway, a man named Gerhard Henrik Armauer Hansen, had isolated the leprosy bacillus, or rod-shaped bacterium, on a laboratory slide. The bacillus was labeled *Mycobacterium leprae*. Still, Dr. Hansen could not stimulate the growth of *Mycobacterium leprae* in the laboratory or determine its reaction to medication, heat, cold, or air. Treatment for the disease remained extremely limited. A box marked Rayne's pills was shipped to the settlement from Honolulu, but the pills had scant effect on the lepers. Damien also received assortments of Hoang-nan pills from a priest in Trinidad. Hoang-nan was a Chinese extract of a poisonous species of ivy. It waged a brief but losing battle against the leprosy bacillus.

By this time, one thousand people were exiled to Kalawao settlement. An epidemic had been declared. Damien comforted the dying with the promise of God's love and forgiveness. He could call each leper by name, and he never forgot a biscuit or treat for the suffering children. After one of his favorite lepers died, he wrote of the young man to Pamphile. In the throes of death, the man had repeated the words of St. Paul: "I desire to be dissolved and to be with Christ." The body was tenderly buried by Damien "under the shadow of the great cross I have erected in the middle of our cemetery. With him lie hundreds of other lepers."

When a new king, Kalakaua, took control of the Sandwich Islands, a royal tour was made of the world. Everywhere King Kalakaua mentioned the settlement on Molokai and asked for charity for the lepers and their *haole* priest. Upon the king's return, and with the intervention of the French consul, the Board of Health was ordered to remove the ban on Damien's activities. The Board gave Damien permission to receive visitors on Molokai and leave the island, yet it criticized him so severely to the Sacred Hearts Mission that a Father Fouesnel of the Mission penned a note to Paris denouncing the priest for his "indiscreet zeal."

Damien's zeal and obstinacy were now focused on constructing cottages at Kalawao. For his lepers he had become beggar, banker, merchant, carpenter, architect, doctor, undertaker, and errand boy. To secure supplies for the cottages, he'd written dozens of letters describing how the lepers crawled about in the open, assaulted by flies and hungry vermin. "Half of the sick," Damien wrote, "are living corpses that worms have begun to devour, at first internally, then externally, leaving the most loathsome wounds, which very rarely heal. To get the idea of the stench they exhale, imagine a coffin full of putrefaction suddenly opened before you."

The majority of Kalawao's lepers had entrusted Damien with their six-dollars-per-year allotment used to order goods from Honolulu, but the sum was not sufficient for materials to build cottages. The Board of Health would have to subsidize the rest of the supplies. "I ask you," Damien wrote in exasperation to the Board, "to send on to me the lumber, nails, tacks, and paint, a detailed order for which you will find enclosed herewith."

Grudgingly the Board members signed a requisition. Damien and a crew of lepers raked several miles of land, and by the time lumber was dumped ashore Damien had a full set of inked sketches. He would lay the floorboards over solid trestles and protect the outer shells by a coat of paint. Enough land had been cleared for three hundred structures, scores of them to be built by Damien himself. He labored under a tropical sun and, like someone possessed, passed his sweat-stained mallets, chisels, and hammers among whatever helpers he had. Better that the sick be quickly housed than that he hoard his collection of tools for worry that they might be contaminated.

The lepers at Molokai were encouraged by Damien to plant vegetable gardens near the cottages and to grow sunflowers and lilies. Potatoes were harvested and charged by the merchant Damien to the Government, earning money for the colony. Damien also fashioned flutes, fifes, and drums from metal kerosene cans and pipes, and he organized a band and choir. Hearing of these improvements, the nuns at the Sacred Hearts Mission sewed silk and cotton costumes, and Honolulu citizens collected alms for Kalawao. Wonder of wonders, the *Kilauea* dropped off clothes, bugles, flutes, trombones, clarinets, drums, flags, and money for Damien to buy egg-laying chickens and a stable of horses for his less crippled parishioners.

Every evening at twilight the choir and band

dressed up to perform at St. Philomena's church. They learned to march in step while singing at the daily funerals. Damien was the bandmaster and choir leader, and the lepers played their music to the echoing roar of the surf. Some of the ill lacked three or four fingers, yet they handled the musical instruments with incredible skill. A visitor to the settlement wrote that the defiled creatures in the band had faces puckered like huge melons and eyelids that curled upward. Pieces of rotted lips sometimes disintegrated from the press of instruments. One woman's ears dangled in a fanlike shape to her shoulders. A young boy carried a brightly colored flag though his back was eaten away to the spinal column, exposing the tip of a blackened lung.

By the early 1880's, Damien had brought a miraculous transformation to Kalawao settlement. The corpse tomb was a living community, prevailing despite its shackles of death and disease. Despair was replaced by a sense of usefulness and meaning. Public games were organized, as were religious holidays and feast days. Damien opened a tiny store, selling at ridiculously low prices or giving away free cooking utensils, biscuits, rice, bread, eggs, and chickens. The wooden cottages were painted white, and Damien had remodeled the dilapidated hospital, installing cots and persuading five of the lepers to work as nurses. He still doctored the patients without help from a physician, but somehow he eked out the hours to build a church at Kalaupapa. Four hundred lepers received Holy Communion from their Makua Kamiano, their Father Damien. A communal saying of the rosary was conducted at weekday Mass, and joyful children, oblivious now to the seal of early death upon their features, assisted as acolytes.

Damien was not just priest and father to the Catholic lepers. He was father to all at the settlement, and his lepers surrounded him after supper, vying for the chance to drink tea from his six battered cups. Having cleared a site next to the crowded graveyard, he built a larger presbytery, its outside staircase winding to a second floor. There, in the putrefied air, he listened to his lepers tell him their legends or answered their questions about his life before he'd come to them. He spoke of Belgium and of his parents, sisters, and brothers. And as he talked, he urged his charges to believe that they were not worthless outcasts. They could live their lives, he told them, with dignity and respect.

An honorary medal was bestowed on Damien by the sister of King Kalakaua, and a tribute to him was written for a Hawaiian newspaper. "In this young priest, Father Damien," said the newspaper, "we see again the heroism of the martyrs in the bloody arenas of the ancient world. His heroism is even greater, for would it not be a greater favor to be thrown to savage beasts than to spend one's life in a leper settlement?"

Damien sent his thanks for the royal medal, but he put it away and did not wear it. The Hawaiian newspaper vanished from the settlement store. Damien had never sought tributes or praise. His work on Molokai sprang from the solitary depths of his commitment to his faith. When a monthly publication of the Sacred Hearts was sent from Europe, bearing a reprint of one of his letters to his mother, he instantly wrote home. "I want," he said, "to remain unknown to the world."

At Kalawao, Damien had the satisfaction of his family of lepers and of the work that, in his own estimation, was never finished. Always there would be more to build and to accomplish. If he was lonely at times, he was able to refresh and renew himself. Even the animals of Molokai responded to him. An American professor named Charles Warren Stoddard, curious about the remarkable settlement of lepers, had visited Damien and vividly recorded an instance of this response. Damien, wrote professor Stoddard, had "brought from his cottage into the churchyard a handful of corn, and scattering a little of it upon the ground he gave a peculiar cry. In a moment his fowls flocked from all quarters; they seemed to descend out of the air in clouds; they lit upon his arms, and fed out of his hands, they fought for footing upon his shoulders and even upon his head; they covered him with caresses and with feathers. He stood . . . among as fine a flock of fowls as any fancier would care to see. They were his pride, his playthings. . . ."

The fowls, scratching about on the ground of what once was the corpse tomb, the desolate prison, had become like Damien's other "flock" of cherished lepers, a part of his family on Molokai. Both flocks were sustained by his caring, by the gritty vigilance of his love.

Chapter

The eight Sandwich Islands of the South Pacific had evolved into a way station for fleets of ships and steamers. Hawaii was used as a naval base, and all the islands had begun to be referred to as Hawaii, the Hawaiian Islands, or the Crossroads of the Pacific. Foreign dignitaries from Europe, North America, Siam, China, and Japan visited King Kalakaua and dined in formal dress at Honolulu's royal mansion.

The port of Honolulu was more sophisticated than before, and sailors beguiled the women with scented soaps and handkerchiefs instead of toys.

A sugarcane industry had become established in the islands, and white men settled in droves on Hawaii, Oahu, and Maui, amassing fortunes from sugar. In the 1870's a commercial treaty was signed between the Hawaiian Islands and the United States, and by the 1880's American businessmen had gained control of important positions in King Kalakaua's court.

Hawaii was increasingly drawn into the commercial and political arena of the white man's world. Communications improved as sailing ships gave way, in the late 1800's, to speedier steamers, and with the perfecting of the wireless telegraph in 1896 the link between Europe, North America, and Hawaii grew stronger. Yet despite these advances, humanity had not managed to decipher the mysterious causes of leprosy or to discover a cure. In Africa, India, China, and South America, the disease was on the uprise, and hundreds of thousands of lepers were still the most repugnant of outcasts. No longer were there havens such as the lazar houses of the Middle Ages. Lepers in Asia were banished to the wilds or segregated in colonies filthier than Kalawao had been in its beginning days.

91

Segregation remained the sole method of reducing the spread of leprosy. Outcasts became the prisoners of their governments and of their own devastated bodies. Some Hawaiians still hid in the hills from police, and *haole* industrialists with suspected leprosy could buy their way out of the islands, but segregation continued. A Hawaiian official, an American named Walter Murray Gibson, allotted funds for a leper hospital on Honolulu's waterfront. The hospital was supposed to be a fine diagnostic treatment center for lepers on the route to Kalawao. In truth, Kakaako Hospital was nothing of the sort; it was overcrowded, rat-infested, and mired in the damp heat of a tract of marshland. Opened by the Board of Health in 1880, it was dismantled at their order in 1888. Before the demise, the Sacred Hearts Mission became involved enough to recruit a nursing staff of nuns from the European order of the Franciscan Sisters of Charity.

The Government of the Hawaiian Islands collected high taxes on the profitable sugar industry, but the revenue went to projects other than Kalawao. If Damien had not nagged the members of the Board of Health, progress at the settlement would have bogged down. A rutted path connected Kalaupapa, where cottages had been built, to Kalawao, and Damien wanted to pave the three-mile distance. The Board agreed to order materials and to issue funds to hire workers, but they negligently delayed shipments. "It was understood," Damien wrote indignantly in English, "that I was to receive $300 for this work. Will you be so kind as to send me what is due *as of today*; namely, $155.20. And this is not all. You know the dangerous rocks that lie off the landing stage. Mr. Meyer and I have just gone down to look them over. It would require dynamite to remove them. I should also require some barrels of cement. Sincerely yours, Damien, Catholic priest."

Before R. W. Meyer submitted his next report on Kalawao settlement, a road was hardened over the old pathway and the rocks at the landing area had been demolished.

Damien's efforts to improve the leper colony brought more frequent appearances of the steamer *Kilauea*. He built two wooden orphanages for the forty leprous children whose parents lived on the other islands, and an elderly widow of a leper acted as matron and cook. Damien put up a school for the children and arranged for several of the adults to teach classes. Boys and girls studied at tables, listened to stories, or practiced needlework to keep them alert. They adored their Makua Kamiano and tagged after him on his rounds. As irascible as he was with authorities and their "fiscal allotments," Damien was endlessly gentle toward the leper children. Many would not have been recognizable to mothers or fathers. Eyes were shrunken or blinded from deterioration; mouths and ears had collapsed and the skin of young bodies was covered with a thick scum of infection. "I found one of my children dying," Damien wrote to Pamphile. "She begged me to bring her the Holy Viaticum. . . . Yesterday I made her coffin myself and dug her grave."

By the year 1881, Damien had seen over 1400 lepers die. Anointing the body, receiving the last confession, praying and offering the Holy Viaticum, the sacred wafer of the last rites, Damien eased the transition from earth for those who had been in agony. Leprosy invaded the lungs, causing asthma and hemorrhage, and the death spasms of a leper could hurl a gush of rancid blood into Damien's face. Along with his holy oil and breviary, he carried a metal basin and towel.

St. Philomena's church was enlarged by Damien, and he attached a loud bell to its steeple to announce Mass and Vespers. A priest in Rome sent sacramental vessels and statuary to adorn the church, but Damien had to dig trenches in the floor so that the lepers could have receptacles in which to cough and spit. One Christmas eve, appraising the church interior, he wrote Pamphile: "Finishing touches on decorating the altar. I'm only half satisfied, since I have only old ornaments to put on it. A mouse in the closet ate big holes in my antependium [altar covering]."

In the sixteen years that Damien lived among the lepers, he was away from the settlement for a mere six months in total. He appeared to be present everywhere and all at once. He was the vortex of energy that had transformed Kalawao. The neat rows of white cottages and tidily pruned gardens, the attention to hygiene that lessened secondary infections such as pneumonia and tuberculosis, the chatter and song at Damien's hospital, orphanages, school, and general store, the proud display of road and churches, of costumes and band instruments and community celebration, proclaimed the revival of Damien's lepers into human beings who hoped more than despaired, who laughed more than they wept, who had learned to live in the midst of a hideous illness that carried the prospect of a gruesome death.

A procession in honor of the Blessed Sacrament was organized by Damien, and visitors were invited from Oahu to share in the celebration. A few accepted and were amazed and moved to find a scene of startling beauty, a panoply of color laid over the dreariness of disease. Twenty new curtains had arrived from Honolulu for St. Philomena's windows, and from the old curtains women in the settlement sewed sashes and long-sleeved vestments and ori-flammes, large devotional banners. On the day of the procession, the church altars at Kalawao and Kalaupapa were decorated with sprays of flowers.

Damien led his troupe of lepers. Little girls of the colony hid their ravaged faces from the strangers, and the choir's leprous vocal cords produced a rasping chant. While men and women were visibily in pain as they staggered forward on the ulcerated stumps of legs or crawled trembling on bandaged knees, they were united in an act of reverence. Dressed in red cassocks with flowing surplices of lace, they struggled to acknowledge Christ's own sacrifice on His fateful journey toward crucifixion upon the hill at Calvary. Centered in the line of worshipers were four men in green satin coats emblazoned with white crosses. They carried a wooden tabernacle on a bamboo platform, gilded doors locked over the Eucharist, the Host of the Blessed Sacrament. The band played its trumpets, bugles, and clarinets, and the procession wound its impressive way from Kalawao to Kalaupapa. For the observers the experience was one that they could never forget and that they would speak of in awe to their families and friends.

Later Damien showed his visitors around the settlement. "We lepers," he said at one point, indicating how close he had become to his "children." Praising the priest and the procession, the men and women of Oahu left Molokai on a special steamer, confident in the knowledge that only prolonged contact with leprosy seemed to transmit the disease.

Damien accompanied his guests to the landing pier and waved at them until the boat was a speck on the horizon. It was 1881, and he was past his fortieth birthday. No longer was he a young priest, wide-eyed and untested. He had toiled for eight years at Kalawao without anyone else from the priesthood. In the past months, he'd admitted to himself that he would like to share his daily joys and vexations. He anticipated the arrival of his occasional visitors. He regretted that they could not stay with him. In his letters to Father Vincke, he asked suddenly for a companion, a compadre of the Sacred Hearts. To Pamphile, with whom he'd truly wanted to divide his mission, he said rashly, "My hands are not in as good condition as yours—you who have nothing to do but page through books."

Father Pamphile, his superiors decided, was of most benefit in Louvain, not at Kalawao. Instead, a Dutchman named André Burgermann was sent to Damien. Burgermann had served his priesthood in Tahiti but had contracted elephantiasis, character- ized by extreme swelling of bodily tissue. At first,

Burgermann was put in charge of the southern section of Molokai, leaving Damien free to spend all his hours at the colony. Damien, however, exchanged districts with the other priest just long enough to build a church, a school, and a presbytery across the *pali*.

André Burgermann was a restless and irritable man. He showed more interest in experimenting with pills and potions to cure himself than in attending to work. Damien tried to like his companion—especially after Burgermann was transferred to Kalaupapa—but the relationship became impossible. The Dutchman told Damien that he wanted the paid position of deputy superintendent under R. W. Meyer and would seek release from his vows. Astonished, Damien stopped confessing to him. In the spring of 1881, Burgermann was recalled to Honolulu for "a certain independence of behavior in the matter of religious poverty," and Damien wrote to Father Vincke and the superior general, "You can no longer count on him. . . . Send me a good son of the congregation, not a pigheaded gentleman."

The second helper assigned to Molokai was Father Albert Montiton, a Frenchman from Normandy who also had served in Tahiti and was afflicted with elephantiasis. The officials of the Sacred Hearts, in releasing a priest to Damien, must have scoured their ranks for men who were already ill. Montiton was three and a half years older than Damien, and he wasted no time remarking that Father Damien "lacked judgment" in exposing himself so closely to leprosy. Damien insisted that his actions were his own business, and the conflict between Montiton and Damien was off to a rousing start.

It was September, 1881, when Albert Montiton unpacked his bags at Kalawao settlement. Damien was accustomed to having unquestioned control over his lepers. His stubbornness and his bluntness were not wild myths invented by the Board of Health. Yet if he was not tactful in speaking to Montiton, the French priest could also be arrogant and ill-humored. He wanted Damien to provide a gate for the new cemetery at Kalaupapa and, when it was mounted, demanded a more ornate design. Damien balked and Montiton was furious. For two weeks, he refused to say Mass at Kalaupapa, so that Damien had to do it, and he reprimanded Damien for dispensing gifts from Oahu to lepers who were living together unmarried. All the lepers, Damien argued, deserved to be treated kindly.

Relief for Damien came in 1884, when Montiton's elephantiasis worsened and he went to Honolulu to consult a doctor. He was greased and bandaged, but the other priests at the Sacred Hearts

Mission where he was staying did their best to avoid him. Disease was not a customary guest at the Mission, and besides Montiton was apt to pester and annoy. In a letter to Paris, Father Léonor Fouesnel wrote that Montiton "looks like a man who has been skinned . . . his ointment, a grease with a very disagreeable smell, does not stop him from being all over us, touching everything, greasing everything. The fathers have fled from him. . . ."

Montiton returned to Kalawao settlement, and Damien hiked to the shore to welcome him. Word arrived, however, that the French priest, like André Burgermann, would be removed from Molokai. Bishop Maigret had considered Father Albert's qualifications. A more suitable assignment was being arranged.

Damien was far from happy. For reasons that he did not tell, he begged Bishop Maigret to reconsider "taking Father Albert from me." The bishop could not be dissuaded. For Damien's own good and for the good of the Mission, Albert Montiton would board the *Kilauea* and resume his post on Tahiti.

On a February morning in 1885, the *Kilauea* moored off the pier at Kalaupapa. Montiton's suitcases were in a rickety wheelbarrow, and the moment of departure had come, but the priest would not speak to Damien. A rowboat, manned by a sailor, bumped at the pier and the suitcases were piled onto one of the roughened seats. Over the water, the sky looked nearly colorless, and birds coasted toward the foam-lapped shore. The rowboat, its two occupants mute, was spun in the direction of the steamer. Damien called out to Montiton, but his call was lost in a strident blast of the *Kilauea*'s whistle.

In less than an hour, the rowboat and its cargo had been swallowed up by the larger vessel. Glancing above him, Damien beheld the labyrinth of cliffs that seemed to burst from Molokai's shoreline. Had those impenetrable walls entombed him without his awareness? No, no, they had not. He had climbed them and conquered them. They had been his challenge and not his prison.

But his left leg? His foot? Was he to be imprisoned now by his body? Surely he was imagining and was as robust as usual. Surely the pain that chafed lately if he walked from the presbytery was only from a sciatic nerve. His foot burned inside his boot at that very moment, and it awakened him at night. But undoubtedly it was a temporary bother. Wasn't it?

Cautiously Damien stepped from the deserted pier to a flat wedge of stone on the pebbled shore. He sank to his knees though he did not pray for any sign. He would find out the answer soon enough. He could pray, he realized, to recapture the resilience of his youth. Or he could pray that Father Albert might sail back to help him or that his lepers —"we lepers"—would find salvation for their souls. But Damien did not pray in actual words. Tears, always the recourse of others, poured down his cheeks. A slash of pain seized his foot. Yet it was wrong, he had said, to attach oneself too closely to the things of the world. One's time on earth was a time of waiting, of exile from eternal peace.

Chapter

Damien was a leper at last.

He was not certain when the disease first struck him. Possibly it had entered his system years earlier —after dressing a gaping wound on one of his lepers, or breathing the fetid air of the cemetery, or sharing a dish of *poi* with his children at eventide, at what they called the "time-of-peace-between-night-and-day." Damien's face and legs had itched on occasion at Kohala, long before he had come to Molokai, and dry patches of skin blotched his body in the 1870's, but the spots somehow disappeared. In 1880, a visiting doctor routinely examined Damien and found him to be nonleprous. Thus, the pain that attacked his left leg and foot had fooled him for a while, had not claimed much of his notice.

Increasingly, the pain and the slight dragging of his foot signaled what Damien described as "the secret poison which threatens to poison the whole body." He was not wholly convinced of his fate until the night that he soaked his feet in a pan of hot water. Home from rounds of the settlement, he heated water over a kerosene stove. His feet ached from all the walking, and he put the pan, steam rising from its edges, on the floor by a chair. Sitting, he unlaced his boots, slipped them off, and lowered his feet into the liquid. He let the warmth radiate through him, and a minute or two passed before he saw the red welts on his toes and ankles.

Damien lifted his feet onto the floor, and gathering up his cassock he examined the burned and blistered flesh. Leaning toward the pan, he lightly touched the tip of a thumb to the water, recoiling at the sting. He must have heated the water to the boiling point, and it had scalded his feet. But he'd not *felt* the burn, except for his thumb. He closed his eyes and nodded. A familiar symptom, the numbness. "Pain occurring in a limb, followed by insensitivity or anesthesia of the nerves." Leprosy. Scourge of the ages. Death before death.

A German bacteriologist, Eduard Arning, was studying leprosy in Honolulu. The doctor had read Gerhard Hansen's experiments on the disease and was trying to culture *Mycobacterium leprae* in the living tissue of monkeys. Arning hoped to trace the exact means by which leprosy passed from one person to another. A convicted murderer in Honolulu had allowed him to implant leprous tumors into a right forearm, but the bacillus did not multiply. The doctor traveled to Kalawao settlement to collect case histories. He held Father Damien in the highest esteem.

Eduard Arning was ushered through the settlement by Damien. Inside the presbytery, however, the tour came to a sudden end. "I believe I am a leper," Damien said. He requested an examination from Arning, reciting his symptoms and delivering himself up to a diagnosis. His skin was scrutinized under the flame of a kerosene lamp, and the pattern of numbness along his leg and foot was probed with a platinum needle. Dr. Arning was silent and pale.

"You will not upset me," Damien reassured his visitor. "I am glad there is no further doubt."

Arning, more in awe of the priest than ever and of his sacrifice at Kalawao, emptied a bottle of pills into a dish. "Arsenica pills," Arning said. "They contain measures of a poison that may bring temporary relief."

For some months the news of Damien's leprosy was guarded within the Sacred Hearts Mission. Bishop Maigret, grieved by the diagnosis, wrote a letter of friendship to Damien. The aging bishop retired from his duties and was replaced by a man named Koeckemann. Father Léonor Fouesnel became the Mission's vice provincial under a provincial who handled administrative duties for the bishop. Both Koeckemann and Fouesnel had monitored reports on Kalawao settlement. Whether they felt that they operated in Damien's shadow, or whether personal jealousies interfered, neither Bishop Koeckemann nor Fouesnel was kindly disposed toward Damien. If asked to comment on the priest's illness, they shrugged. Of course Father Damien had been of service to the Mission. Of course the lepers would be losing their earthly servant. But no priest of the islands, they said, should be singled out; no priest should be venerated for simply performing at his post.

Damien sent a letter to his mother and brothers in Tremeloo, but he never mentioned his illness. His mother, widowed for thirteen years, was almost eighty-three, and he feared that she might not survive a shock. He wrote of burning his feet and having to ride about in a horse-drawn cart, but he said he was feeling better. In stilted French, for he'd forgotten most of his native Flemish, he commented: "I don't change much apart from my beard which is turning gray. . . . So, in the midst of my sick people, I play at being sick myself."

To Pamphile, Damien spelled out the truth, cautioning him to keep the confidence. For once, he did not urge his brother to serve at Kalawao. "Our good God," he said, "has fixed your residence in our native country." As for his leprosy, it had been "anticipated from my first arrival" on Molokai.

By 1886, when Damien was showing the obvious effects of his disease, reports of him leaked across the oceans. Newspapers seized on the account of the Catholic priest who'd sequestered himself for nearly fourteen years among the most odious of the ill. Society had shunned its lepers, but one man— Father Damien de Veuster of Belgium—had provided what others would not, had stepped forward when others retreated. Now Damien, too, was ill. At the age of forty-six, he would be mutilated and destroyed by the scathing sword of disease.

In Belgium, a neighbor of the de Veusters read

a newspaper and told Anne-Catherine that her son was a leper and that his skin was falling in pieces from his body. The exaggerated story convinced the mother that her son was at death's door. She had saved each of Damien's letters. The photograph of him taken before he'd left Louvain was on the wall by her bed. Clutching her packet of letters, Anne-Catherine prayed for the son who'd renounced the life of a grain merchant for the calling of a priest. "Well, then," she whispered to her family, "Joseph and I shall go together." And on the afternoon of April 5, 1886, Damien's mother was dead.

At Kalawao that summer, Damien prayed for the souls of his parents. A Father Beissel came from Maui to hear his confession, but eighteen months had elapsed since Albert Montiton sailed to Tahiti, and Damien was without a helpmate. He tried to estimate how much time might be left to him. A year? Perhaps two? Physicians graphed the life-span of a leper at from three to fifteen years. In Damien's case, not only were his limbs numb, but his right ear oozed with a blistered tumor, and his voice was muffled and raspy from the destruction of his larynx.

In the month of July, he saw the *Kilauea* approaching Kalaupapa pier and he limped down to the shore. He leaned on a wooden piling while a dry trade wind whipped the brim of his string-tied hat.

A rowboat edged toward him, a rope was looped over the piling, and a stranger climbed from the forward seat. "Father Damien," the man said, "I have come to work. I am Ira Joseph Dutton."

He was pleasant looking, the brown-haired man in the denim suit. He'd been born in the United States, he explained, in the state of Vermont and had fought in the Civil War. He'd married badly, was divorced, and had converted to Catholicism. At a Trappist monastery, he was an oblate, a layman without vows, but he wanted a more active life. He went to New Orleans where he happened upon an article about Father Damien. To work on Molokai was what he desired.

"I've obtained permission," Dutton said, carefully unfolding letters of consent and approval from Bishop Koeckemann and the Board of Health.

"Are you willing," Damien interrupted, "to make a vow that you will stay here for at least a year?"

"I am," Dutton replied.

"Do you know that I am a leper?"

"I do," Dutton answered.

"Then come along," Damien said.

Ira Joseph Dutton, dubbed Brother Joseph by Damien, would stay not just one year at Kalawao settlement. He worked on Molokai for forty-four years, recording daily events in a lengthy and valuable memoir. Damien built him a one-room house near the presbytery and put him in charge of the boys' orphanage. A kinship sprang up between them at the moment of meeting, though—or perhaps because—Dutton's style and personality were in stark contrast to the priest's. As Damien was outspoken, Dutton was restrained. As Damien was oblivious to rips in his faded cassock, Dutton was trim and neatly dressed, his house tidy, his blankets rolled in military order on his mat.

With Dutton to help him, Damien set forth on a frenzied whirl of remodeling and construction. The boys' and girls' orphanages were widened, and a common kitchen was built. Damien's complexion had darkened to the telltale ruddiness of a leper and the knuckles on his hands cracked into purulent ulcers, yet his fingers were agile and he used them as if they were tools on brief loan. A doctor tardily assigned to Kalawao by the Board of Health suggested that Damien rest, but the advice was greeted by a snort. "Rest?" Damien said. "I intend to die in harness. It's no time to rest now, when there is so much to do and my time is so short!"

His leprosy, his "secret poison," was as the ancient battlefields of Damien's childhood games. All his reserves were attuned to acting, to doing—always, always to doing. He wheedled money and materials

110

from the Board of Health to establish a water supply at Kalaupapa. Six yoke of oxen were ordered to haul the pipes. He constructed wooden dining halls for his lepers, and he assembled eating tables and benches. He would plan one project, start another, and move to a third, relying on Dutton to wind up loose ends. "I am the carpenter," he said, "and Brother Joseph the joiner."

Somehow he found the hours to frolic with the girls and boys, and he would jolt across a grassy tongue of land by the hospital, his laughter trailing behind him, the gnomelike children in a gleeful chase. Mouritz, the settlement doctor, wrote that Damien still tended his fowls. He clucked at them to flutter over his shoulders, and often he picked up a downy chick and held it in one palm like an admired jewel.

Yet he was growing weaker. By January, 1887, tumors invaded his arms, chest, and back. The mucous membranes of his nose and throat were pitted with disease, and his cheeks and left ear were excessively swollen. He felt in great need of confession and decided to go to Kakaako Hospital in Honolulu. He could investigate a new treatment of baths for lepers, and he might ask for confession from Bishop Koeckemann. Oahu was only four hours away.

Damien requested permission for the trip from Bishop Koeckemann. "A week or two is all I will require," he said, but at the bishop's bidding the return mail carried a rejection from Vice Provincial Fouesnel. Damien, in all "delicacy" and "charity," should stay where he belonged, Fouesnel had said.

Superintendent Meyer rushed to Damien's defense and pleaded his case in letters to Paris and Louvain. Leprosy, according to recent medical journals, was not contagious in short exposures. Why shouldn't Damien go to Honolulu? "Always have unshakable courage," the superior general wrote his leper priest, overruling the travel objections of the Mission. Damien could admit himself to Kakaako Hospital, but he also received another message from Léonor Fouesnel. "It's as if," Fouesnel sniped, "we have nothing but Molokai and its lepers. If you go to Kakaako, you will not be allowed to say Mass in the chapel there, for neither Father Clément nor I would say Mass with the chalice and vestments you had used, and the sisters would refuse Holy Communion from your hand."

Fouesnel's letter was more painful to Damien than any agonies he ever endured. Whatever hardships he'd tackled, he'd tackled willingly. Obstacles were to be met, and isolation had been an opportunity to work without distraction. His leprosy itself had not

112

overwhelmed him emotionally. But the letter from Léonor Fouesnel ostracized Damien from the Sacred Hearts Mission. He'd thought of himself as a laborer for his church. If the bishop and Fouesnel dismissed him as a priest, he was without underpinnings.

Damien boarded the *Kilauea* at its next visit and sailed the fifty-two miles to Honolulu. A room had been lovingly prepared for him by the Franciscan Sisters. To the nuns and their mother superior, Mother Marianne, Damien was a hero. Fouesnel's warning that they would refuse Holy Communion was deliberately false. Damien was the one who'd inspired the sisters to leave their European cloisters for Oahu's marshland. Each nun contributed to the room set aside for Damien—a patchwork quilt, a bowl of tiny orchids in the red soil of the tropics, a plate of fresh cranberries and mangos. Sister Antonella whitewashed the walls and hung pictures. Mother Marianne placed her own crucifix on a hook above the bed.

Not since his monastery years in Louvain had Damien enjoyed the cool luxury of sheets. The sisters waited on him hand and foot, and as if to make up for his bouts of loneliness, he talked incessantly to them of Molokai. Their services, he said, would be a blessing to the settlement. Couldn't one or two sisters return with him? They smiled and warmed cups of peppermint tea for him and promised that they would speak to the Board of Health.

Bishop Koeckemann, Eduard Arning, and Walter Murray Gibson, now prime minister of the islands, visited Damien at Kakaako Hospital. The bishop heard Damien's confession, and Gibson brought month-old newspaper stories of world events that had not reached Kalawao. The United States had been talking of annexation of the Hawaiian Islands. Casually Gibson referred to rumors of *haole* revolution in Honolulu. Protestants were demanding that King Kalakaua's powers be constitutionally reduced and that the pro-Catholic Gibson resign. Later that year, on June 30, a quick and bloodless revolution did indeed remove Honolulu's court, and Gibson fled to San Francisco.

Damien followed a regimen of baths in his two weeks at Kakaako Hospital. The bathing was prescribed by a Dr. Goto, of Japan, who'd been hired by the Board of Health. Dr. Goto roamed the halls of the ramshackle hospital to supervise the twice-daily bathing of patients. According to Damien, "a certain decoction of tisane made from Japanese tree bark" and a Japanese medication were added to bath water of 108 degrees. The baths were thought to reduce the misery of leprous symptoms and to slow the progression of the disease.

114

At the end of the two weeks, Damien said that he felt rejuvenated and energetic. He was anxious to return to Molokai and to ask the Board of Health about adding the Goto baths to the settlement. None of the sisters had been granted entry to Kalawao, but they wrapped up sheets and comforters for Damien to bring his lepers. Mother Marianne accompanied the priest to the dock where the *Kilauea* was loading. In four hours, Damien told the gentle-faced nun, he would be home, he would be happy.

On Molokai, he did not slow his frenzied pace. He badgered the Board of Health for money and supplies for a larger hospital, a boiler room, two fully equipped bathhouses, a cookhouse, another dining hall, a dispensary, and six dormitories. He ordered fifty boxes of Dr. Goto's Kai Gio Kioso Yoku Yaku medicine, fifty boxes of Sei Kets-uren pills, fifty packages of Decoction Hichiyon bark, and ten pounds of Sodium bicarbonate. The board shipped the medication but refused to pay for Damien's "grandiose plans," so Damien, Dutton, and several lepers cut down kukui trees for wood, built a bathhouse, and converted large metal bread boxes into tubs. Superintendent Meyer shipped a ton of coal for heating the tubs, and Damien instituted a daily schedule of baths.

He was convinced that he saw a drop in the death

rate at Kalawao, but he was overly optimistic. The Goto baths were primarily a calming treatment. If overused, they could be dangerous. Damien himself spent too many hours in the heated water. He thought that he was less lame and that the pus-filled tumors on his right hand were healing, but the resident physician reported a different story. Damien, Dr. Mouritz said, had been exhausted by the Goto baths. He was tottering about the settlement, his cassock "hanging off him like a bag," his face hideously swollen and his body shrunken over a mass of crippled bones.

Damien was grossly and irreversibly ill. Had he left Molokai, he could have embarked on a final journey aboard the *Kilauea* to the merciful care of the sisters at Kakaako Hospital. But he would not remove his "harness," nor would he allow the deadly reins of his leprosy to check the fervor of his days. "I would refuse," he wrote, "to be cured if my departure from the island and abandoning all my work here were to be the price."

Damien's work, his all-embracing ardor, was the strongest salve upon any of Kalawao settlement's unsparing horrors.

Chapter 9

The voice of the bell on St. Philomena's called the lepers to Mass, and all across the world the name of Damien de Veuster resounded in its own timbre. Few men in history had dared to come so close to leprosy. Damien had caught the dreaded disease, and in so doing he captured the curiosity of millions. News about him made frequent headlines in newspapers in the United States and Europe, and the

Mission in Honolulu was besieged with letters inquiring for his health or suggesting cures for his illness. Church ornaments were shipped to Damien from a pastor in Boston, Massachusetts, and from an archbishop in Portland, Oregon. An Irish working girl in Massachusetts sent the whole of her savings, and a newspaper in Berlin proclaimed: "Voyagers of all nations, salute when you pass the cliffs of Molokai."

In London, a committee was formed to collect funds for Kalawao settlement. The head of the committee was the Reverend Mr. Hugh Chapman, vicar of St. Luke's Church, Camberwell. Mr. Chapman wrote Damien that "the story of your life has taught me more than the books I have read." Though the vicar was an Anglican supporting a Roman Catholic, which prompted criticism from outraged Protestants, the contributions for Father Damien and his lepers were surprisingly high. In 1887 and 1888, the London *Times* reserved space for Hugh Chapman's campaign and £2,620 or $13,100 was sent to Kalawao.

The United States outdid England by contributing $28,621, but the money was not a source of joy to the Government of the Hawaiian Islands. If the world supposed that Hawaiian lepers were neglected, then the blame would fall on officials in Honolulu. Wasn't the Board of Health doing its best for the lepers? And if it wasn't—if it never had—must the world *know?* Damien was troublesome, a thorn in the side. Couldn't Bishop Koeckemann keep his disquieting priest in line?

"You have enough glory," the bishop bristled in a letter to Damien. And Léonor Fouesnel directed that all letters written by Damien be sent to the Mission for censoring.

Damien dispensed the money and gifts that accumulated on Molokai to the churches at Kalawao and Kalaupapa and to a bank account for the settlement. When he saw how uplifted the lepers—the *other lepers*—were with the contributions, he was convinced that the donations must be good for Kalawao. Didn't his children need whatever balm could be given them? His superiors had misjudged him. He wanted nothing for himself from outside the colony. In a notebook of jottings and prayers, he expressed his sorrow over the accusations from the Mission. His words from a psalm would later echo throughout continents. *"Non nobis, Domine, non nobis,"* he printed in Latin, *"sed nomine tuo da gloriam."* "Not to us, Lord, not to us, but to thy name give glory."

An April storm blew down the bell and peaked roof on St. Philomena's church, and Damien limped between splintered plants and bent nails. His instinct was to repair the damage, but could he? Did he have the strength? His ears hung in crimson globes, the skin broken and dribbling fluid. His eyesight had been failing, and the bones in his legs were decaying. At month's end, however, he was crouched atop a finished roof, putting in the last nails, and had a crew of leper masons and carpenters to help him with a stone addition.

Damien's illness was not as manageable when he presided over Sunday Mass. He winced at having to offer the wafers to his congregation from hands that were gravely ulcerated. One Sunday, in the midst of a sermon, he toppled to the floor. Gasps shot from the pews, and worshipers lurched forward to lift Damien to his feet. A rim of his spectacles had broken, and the thickened ridges on his forehead were bleeding. "Makua Kamiano," the lepers whispered. "We are with you. We are here."

If only another priest could be sent to the colony to supplement Damien's efforts. "It's the one thing I beg of you," he wrote the Mission. His religious duties might be divided, and Brother Joseph Dutton could oversee Kalawao and Kalaupapa. Months passed without a visit from any priest, and Damien was confessing alone at St. Philomena's altar. Yet a letter received from Léonor Fouesnel did not solve the mounting problems. "Be patient," Fouesnel wrote. "As soon as you are helpless, you will have

120

someone. I have resolved to have nothing more to do with you, until new orders."

Fouesnel, still smarting under Damien's fame, demanded that he draw up his will in favor of the bishop or a successor. The bank money would not belong to the settlement at Damien's death. Fouesnel had asked donors to send funds for Molokai to the Mission rather than to Damien, but the sly maneuver failed. Damien was the one whom the donors trusted. Damien was the one who excited their charity. The priest, not others who lived apart from Molokai, would know what to do for the lepers.

"Be patient," Fouesnel had written. "As soon as you are helpless, you will have someone." Damien, however, was fighting the battle again helplessness. Infection filled his lungs and encumbered his breathing, but even in the profundity of the mortification of his flesh, of crucifixion by dark and racking disease, he would not stop his "doing." Riding in his horse-drawn cart, he made himself visible at each of the 374 buildings and cottages of the settlement. Over 500 lepers were counted on Molokai, with dozens of cases admitted each week. To the non-Catholics, Damien spoke of God, offering them baptism into the faith. To the Catholics, he opened the doors of St. Philomena's, having painted the walls with the splashes of bright color that so attracted the Hawaiians. In spite of his bruising tumble at the altar, he continued Mass and the communal saying of the rosary. "He did not want to stop," Joseph Dutton later remarked, "until he actually fell."

At last, in the autumn of 1888, there were more helpers for Molokai. Father Lambert Conrardy, a Jesuit priest who'd worked among the Indians of Oregon, arrived at Kalaupapa. Conrardy had come to Damien on his own, although the mere sight of the leper priest caused him shattering headaches. Kalawao itself upset Conrardy's stomach. Hens and pigeons pecked at tatters of discarded finger ends in the garbage, and Conrardy was without appetite for meals. Gradually, he grew more accustomed to the settlement. The courage of the sufferers enabled him to forget the ghastly panorama of bloated organs and rotted flesh. Damien himself sometimes forgot his own harrowing illness. He would slip Conrardy an orange or a chunk of candy. "You must eat this," he rasped. "No leper has touched it."

The next helper to land on Molokai was James Sinnett, an Irishman who had traveled the world and lived wildly. Damien called him Brother James and put him to work in the hospital. And in November, to Damien's delight, three nuns were rowed ashore from the *Kilauea.* Damien recognized the beatific smiles of Mother Marianne, Sister Vincentia, and

Sister Leopoldina. The Franciscan nuns arrived to supervise a girls' home at Kalaupapa contributed by a wealthy Hawaiian, a Mr. C. W. Bishop.

The Franciscan sisters swept, dusted, washed, scrubbed, and scoured, and the settlement had never looked as clean. The Bishop Home for Girls was soon ready for occupancy, and the nuns walked to Kalawao to pick up the children at Damien's orphanage. Mother Marianne recounted how Damien stroked the disfigured heads of the girls. "I shall shortly be dead," he told them, "but you won't be left alone. The sisters will take care of you."

Two of the little girls refused to go. In tears, they sank to the ground and clung to Damien's feet. "Please, Father, please," they sobbed. "We want to stay with you until we die." Wearily Damien nodded. The children would have better quarters at Kalaupapa, but how could he resist? The two girls were kept at Kalawao until his death, and only then did they ride in a wagon to the Bishop Home. Not long after, they died in the arms of Mother Marianne.

The last helper to appear at the colony was Father Wendelin Moellers, a German priest of the Sacred Hearts who'd been sent by the Mission. Had Léonor Fouesnel decided that Damien was helpless? Apparently he had. Like Joseph Dutton, Father Wendelin kept a detailed record of his experiences with

Damien, and, like the others who volunteered their services, he grew to feel an abiding love for the ailing priest of the lepers.

Damien's life, his exile on earth, was ebbing away. Sometimes, in his pain, he wondered if Bishop Koeckemann and Léonor Fouesnel were right, if he were unworthy of their respect or of entrance into Heaven. Dr. Mouritz explained that such moments of despair were a common symptom of leprosy and that Damien's optimism was not permanently gone. But whatever his mood in those agonizing days, Damien's suffering was greatly soothed by the volunteers who'd come to aid him. Once he had written to Father Vincke that "the hard thing is to persevere." Now, feeling the cold breath of approaching death, he at least was warmed by companions who cared.

Two weeks into December, the *Kilauea* brought a Christmas visitor to the bustling settlement. The Rev. Mr. Chapman's fund raising in London had alerted a well-to-do English painter named Edward Clifford to the story of Damien and the lepers. Clifford was a Protestant who in childhood was so fearful of Catholics that he'd thought he would be kidnapped by nuns and burned alive. Yet once he heard of Damien's work, he could not put from his mind a visual image of the man. Packing his clothes, his drawing paper, and his charcoals, he left England and took the same route from Europe that Damien had taken in 1864.

Edward Clifford climbed ashore at Kalaupapa with thirteen lepers who'd been sentenced to Molokai. From his wagon, Damien greeted the newcomers and escorted Clifford to a tiny "guesthouse" belonging to the Board of Health. In the Englishman's luggage were articles that had been donated by London patrons—engravings and prints, silver vessels, a magic lantern that displayed slides of distant countries, a watercolor of St. Francis of Assisi that Damien hung in his bedroom.

The priest never stepped over the threshhold of the guesthouse, but he invited his English visitor to the vine-covered presbytery. In the fourteen days of Clifford's stay, while the artist sketched a charcoal portrait of Damien, the two men sat shaded by a blossoming honeysuckle on the wooden balcony of the presbytery. From the yard, lepers sang "Adeste Fideles" in honor of the Christmas season. Young boys scampered or tiptoed up the outside staircase, their blighted faces turned raptly toward Clifford's drawing pad. Again, in the color and song of the settlement, the ugliness of leprosy had been supplanted by a transcending beauty.

Damien and Edward Clifford talked by the hour about Kalawao settlement. The Englishman learned that not everyone was susceptible to leprosy. One woman, Damien said, had lived free of illness at Kalawao with her leper husband. Losing her mate, the woman was twice more married to leprous men and never became ill. Children of lepers, Damien said, were also free of the disease at birth. Whether they contracted leprosy depended on their predisposition and on whether they lived with a stricken parent or parents.

On Christmas day, 1888, Edward Clifford completed his portrait of Damien. The charcoal sketch was a gentle one. In an act of friendship, Clifford had modified the ravaged features of the priest, showing him in profile. No mirrors hung at the settlement, however, and Damien was shocked by his appearance. "What an ugly face!" he barked. "I did not know the disease had made such progress."

Before Clifford ended his visit to Kalawao, he asked Damien to sign the Bible that he'd packed from England. With stumpy fingers, Damien grasped the shaft of a quill pen. His attachment to Edward Clifford went beyond words, but he wrote in a thin and trembling scrawl: "I was sick and ye visited me. J. Damien de Veuster."

On the last day of December, the English painter bid his new friend a sad farewell. Damien rode in the cart to Kalaupapa pier and stood leaning against

James Sinnett's shoulder. Lepers crowded around him, serenading Clifford from the shore. A blast of ship whistle wafted mournfully through the air, and while he gazed at the stark scene before him Edward Clifford resolved, as had Professor Charles Warren Stoddard, to write a remembrance of his visit with Father Damien. The priest, Clifford wrote, had exceeded the limits of most other men. Emaciated and deformed, he stood that day on the rocks with his people "till we slowly passed from their sight. The sun was getting low in the heavens, the beams of light were slanting down the mountainsides, and then I saw the last of Molokai in a golden veil of mist."

Damien, too, was seeing the last of the cliffs and the water-washed pier where he had so often presented himself to say good-bye.

Chapter

The harness tightened further, and by March of 1889 Damien could not move from the presbytery. Leprosy was plundering its spoils. Father Wendelin held Sunday Mass at Kalawao and Kalaupapa and wrote in his diary of the waning hours with the leper priest. Damien's fingers had collapsed back to his knuckles, the bridge of his nose fell in, and he was partially blind. Abscesses on his legs were cleansed and bandaged by James Sinnett, but other abscesses had eaten into his organs. His lungs, bladder, and intestines were infected, and he was coughing up a greenish pus. After nights without sleep, he was assaulted by bouts of stomach pain and diarrhea.

He lay on a straw pallet in the presbytery's upstairs bedroom, insisting in the afternoons that Brother James Sinnett and Father Conrardy carry him down to the front yard. His lepers thronged to his side, chanting to him, whispering, proffering him freshly laid eggs. He permitted no tears from his children. His life had been good, he told them. He missed the settlement, but death could be a peaceful closure to the time spent on earth, to the days, months, or years that were invested in man by God.

Others must "do" now in his place, he told his lepers. Just as years ago he had changed places with his brother Pamphile on the mission to the Sandwich Islands, others would assure that the work was continued when he was gone.

Damien dictated letters printed and sent by Lambert Conrardy to Pamphile, to the Rev. Mr. Hugh Chapman, and to Edward Clifford. Chapman was thanked for his generosity toward the settlement. To Clifford, Damien commented, "I have been steadily yielding the last flickers of vitality." A final letter was written to Pamphile. "Kindly remember me," Damien said from his pallet, "to all the fathers and brothers of Louvain, to Gérard, Léonce, and all the family. . . . Pray and get prayers for me, who am being gently drawn to the grave. May God strengthen me, and give me the grace . . . of a happy death. Your devoted brother, Damien de Veuster."

Conrardy and Sinnett had been sleeping downstairs at the presbytery, and Father Wendelin spent the evenings at Kalaupapa. Each night at 11:45, Damien asked Sinnett to start the prayers for Holy Communion. Conrardy awakened and walked with Sinnett to St. Philomena's to bring Damien the wafer and wine. On the path back to the presbytery, Sinnett lit a torch and rang a small bell. Lepers, both Catholic and non-Catholic, knelt in the cottages in prayer or in homage to their Makua Kamiano.

On March 30, Damien made confession to Father Wendelin. The two priests renewed the vows that bound them to the Congregation of the Sacred Hearts and talked of the hope for greater tolerance among the world religions. After an hour, Damien heard Father Wendelin's confession and, slightly raising his right hand, gave him absolution by tracing the sign of the cross.

130

The following day the leprous sores on Damien's body underwent the crusting over caused by a drying up of fluid as the body ceased to function and produce new cells. It was a sure sign that the end was approaching. In his diary, Wendelin Moellers wrote that the change did not seem to upset Damien. "During the day," Father Wendelin noted, "he was bright and cheerful. 'Look at my hands,' he said. 'All the wounds are healing, and the crust is becoming black—that is a sign of death, as you know very well. . . . I have seen so many lepers die, that I cannot be mistaken. Death is not far off.'"

Conrardy and Sinnett lifted a spare bed into Damien's room but only just managed to talk the priest into lying on it. "How poorly off he was!" Father Wendelin wrote. "He who had spent so much . . . relieving the lepers, had forgotten himself so far as not to have even a change of linen, or sheets for his bed."

A leprosy specialist and a medical photographer from New York traveled to Molokai to compile Damien's case history. Although the sunlight hurt him, Damien asked to be photographed in the yard with some of the boys from his orphanage. A day later he was shaking with fever, and in his last photograph he had been propped up by Conrardy and Sinnett. His eyes stared out from that photograph like sunken holes, and yet there was an ardent quality to his expression, piercing and indelible, the same fire that Father Vincke had seen in the nineteen-year-old Damien at Louvain.

Letters were delivered to Kalawao settlement from every quarter of the world. The Sacred Hearts Mission issued bulletins on Damien's health, and Bishop Koeckemann mellowed enough to send greetings to the priest along with a meerschaum pipe. Vice Provincial Fouesnel remained hostile. "Don't be so positive in your notions," Fouesnel wrote without provocation. "Compose yourself, Father! Be calm . . . and behave as others have done in your plight."

On April 2, the last rites were administered to Damien by Father Lambert Conrardy. Lepers— Damien's lepers—collected in the bedroom and would not be turned away. They were his friends, his mourners, his parishioners, his flock. "It was impossible to chase them out," James Sinnett explained. From the bedside, Father Wendelin asked Damien if, when the time came, he would speak above of those who were left at the settlement. "Yes," Damien rasped, "if I have credit with God, I shall intercede for all who are in the *leprosérie*."

Tearfully Father Wendelin begged the dying priest to leave him his tattered cassock so that Damien's great heart might be inherited, as the prophet Elijah had done for Elisha. "But what would you do with my cassock?" Damien replied, conferring his blessing instead. "It is all full of leprosy."

Death had come to claim Damien's body, but still he would not die. For over a week he lay on the bed, rolled up in a blanket, quivering with fever. Mother Marianne and Sisters Vincentia and Leopoldina visited him, sponging his head with a cool cloth, and the parishioners continued their melancholy vigil in the bedroom. By Saturday, April 13, Damien was in extremis. His temperature had risen to 105 degrees, and his eyelids were so swollen that he could not, with his partial blindness, see the painting of St. Francis on his wall. Shortly after midnight he received Holy Communion for the last time. He slipped in and out of consciousness, whispering to Father Wendelin, "How sweet it is to die a child of the Sacred Hearts."

On Sunday, Father Wendelin spoke to Damien before walking to Kalaupapa to officiate at Mass. Damien could not answer, but affectionately he pressed his compadre's hand. Then, on the following morning, April 15, 1889, a note was delivered to the church at Kalaupapa. Damien was in his agony, Lambert Conrardy had written. Father Wendelin ran from the church but was met on the road by a weeping leper. The message was understood before it could be relayed. Damien was gone. Kamiano was dead. The sores of his leprosy had closed over, and he'd died in James Sinnett's arms as if he "were falling asleep."

It was the Monday of Holy Week, the week before Easter. It was a time for all at the settlement to reflect upon the resurrection of whatever might be eternal. The body of Damien de Veuster had been devoured by disease, but the spirit in him seemed able to reign supreme, to surpass any earthly limitations in order to obtain abiding peace for the soul.

On April 16, Damien's body was carried to St. Philomena's church in a coffin lined by the Franciscan sisters with white satin. Grieving lepers gathered in the church, tears pouring down cankered faces. Outside the sun hung overhead, burnished and remote. Mournfully the residents of Kalawao and Kalaupapa made arrangements for the funeral to be held the next day. The solemn procession that wound along the main road was as colorful and reverent as any Damien himself had ever headed. A crossbearer, dressed in a white soutane, led the choir and band. The sisters walked with the women and girls, followed by the black-draped coffin tenderly placed on the shoulders of eight men. Behind the coffin were Fathers Wendelin and Conrardy, then Joseph Dutton and James Sinnett, and then came the men and boys of the colony.

The funeral oration was given by Father Wendelin. *"Aloha oe, Makua, aloha oe,"* the lepers chanted—"Farewell, Father, farewell"—and the coffin was lowered into a grave whose site had been selected by Damien. He'd asked to rest under the gnarled pandanus tree where he had first slept at Kalawao. It marked a full circle of his life upon the island of Molokai.

In Honolulu, two weeks after the burial, a Pontifical High Mass was sung at the cathedral. Bishop Koeckemann and Léonor Fouesnel were celebrants. Reports of Damien's death had echoed across the world, and tributes were paid to him in thousands of publications. Every town and city with a newspaper featured an article on Father Damien de Veuster. The last photograph of Damien, showing him so disfigured, was pasted in a London shopwindow, and crowds lined up for blocks to see it. Edward Clifford honored his friend at a public meeting, and Hugh Chapman wrote to the London *Times* that new funds for Kalawao should be collected. Another wealthy Hawaiian named H. P. Baldwin contributed a spacious boys' home to the settlement.

Damien's death sparked the founding of a world-wide campaign to find the cure for leprosy. Committees arose in Europe, the Orient, Central America, and the United States, and poets, musicians, novelists, and journalists explored the horrors of leprosy and the moral beauty of Molokai's leper priest. In England, a group of dignitaries formed a committee to establish a Damien Institute for research. Patrons such as the Prince of Wales, Cardinal Manning, and the Archbishop of Canterbury lent their names to the committee and vowed to seek a means of treatment for the many thousands of lepers in India, Africa, China, and the British Empire.

The English committee voted to erect a monument at Kalawao settlement. A granite cross was shipped to Honolulu, and King Kalakaua escorted it to a site near Kalaupapa pier. On the pedestal of the cross was a white marble tablet, inscribed with the words: *Greater love hath no man than this, that a man lay down his life for his friends.*

Above Damien's grave, the Congregation of the Sacred Hearts embedded a black marble cross. It was engraved: *Sacred to the Memory of the Reverend Father Damien de Veuster Died a Martyr to his Charity for the Afflicted Lepers April 15, 1889.* And in Louvain, in 1894, the Belgians raised a bronze monument to their native son.

Damien's few articles of clothing, his box of

tools, his books, and his letters from friends and family were fumigated by Joseph Dutton and sent to Belgium. There they were exhibited in a museum built onto the farmhouse in Tremeloo. Dutton also sent strips of bark from the pandanus tree to anyone who wrote him. Of Kalawao's seven helpers, Dutton left the settlement only once after Damien's death, at the age of eighty-seven when he was critically ill and transferred to a hospital in Honolulu. James Sinnett sailed from Molokai soon after Damien's funeral, feeling lost and unhappy without him. Father Conrardy stayed for six more years until 1895, Father Wendelin remained until 1902, and Mother Marianne died in 1918, having labored at Kalaupapa for thirty years.

The number of lepers in residence at Kalawao settlement was counted at 1,200 in 1889, but the terrible epidemic slowly diminished. In 1912, there were 560 lepers on Molokai and by the 1940's less than 300. Leprosy, however, did not disappear from all the countries of the world. The United States Government staffed a leprosy hospital in Carville, Louisiana, and Dr. Eduard Arning, who'd diagnosed Damien's disease, returned to Europe to establish his research experiments in medical centers.

In 1895, a strange priest landed at Kalaupapa

pier. After years of waiting, Pamphile was assigned to the mission in the Hawaiian Islands. His superiors were disposed to have another Sacred Hearts priest on Molokai and who better, in light of the favorable publicity, than Damien's brother? But Pamphile spent just twenty months at Kalawao. His gesture of love for his brother did not make him a fit missionary. At the age of fifty-eight, he was a learned scholar, a man unaccustomed to life outside the monastery. When fatigue forced his recall to Louvain, where he died twelve years later of a heart attack, he comforted himself with remembering the words that his younger brother had written him. "Our good God has fixed your residence in our native country," Damien had said.

In 1898, the United States annexed the Hawaiian Islands as a territory. The United States Public Health Service established a Leprosy Investigation Station at Kalawao, open to patients on a voluntary basis, in the area where Damien once built his makeshift Goto baths. The American flag flew from the top of the station, and the large rooms were filled with modern equipment and machinery, but the project did not succeed. In an effort to have the settlement closer to a landing pier, the Board of Health had transferred most of the lepers from Kalawao to Kalaupapa. Very few Hawaiians volunteered to be confined in the United States Investigation Station at Kalawao. Damien, whether as symbol or in memory, had taught his children to feel responsible but *free*.

The nineteenth century had become the twentieth century. Thousands of citizens from the United States and other countries were beginning to view the leper as a human being, as someone in need of help, not as a disgusting and untouchable pariah. Damien's sacrifice had dramatized unforgettably the leper's right to human dignity, yet the outcast priest was still a subject of controversy. From the shores of the South Pacific to the stone walls of the Sacred Hearts monasteries in Paris and in Louvain, Damien de Veuster's story had not even approached its end.

Chapter **11**

In the 1880's, Charles McEwen Hyde, a Presbyterian minister from the United States, had been living in Honolulu. Born in New York, Dr. Hyde trained young men for the ministry. Hyde was said to be a strict and inflexible man. He did not speak well of the Hawaiian people or of his peers in the Catholic Church. He had taken a liking to fine food and furnishings, to polished carriages at his door.

140

Damien had died a hero, and a colleague of Hyde's named H. B. Gage had written to the minister to ask about the praise being heaped on the leper priest. By return mail, Hyde curtly replied that Damien "had no hand in the reforms and improvements" at Kalawao, that he "was not a pure man in his relations with women," and that "the leprosy of which he died should be attributed to his vices and carelessness."

"The simple truth," Hyde said of Damien, "is he was a coarse, dirty man."

H. B. Gage sent his colleague's letter to the editors of an Australian newspaper. Yet if Hyde was embarrassed by the furor over his published accusations, he was utterly astonished at the reaction of the renowned and popular writer Robert Louis Stevenson.

Two months after Damien's death, Stevenson had visited Kalawao settlement. Ill with tuberculosis, the author paled at the sights of leprosy's disfigurement. "An infinite pity," he wrote, describing "the mangled limb, the devastated face." Stevenson witnessed what Damien had accomplished at the colony. He interviewed the people, especially the non-Catholics, and he tried to comprehend Damien the man, to see the priest without a halo. Eight days on Molokai convinced Robert Louis Stevenson of Damien's gifts. Here, the author decided, had lived an extraordinary spirit who was also human, a priest whose outbursts of temperament balanced his virtues of character. Here had been a stubborn crusader who was as strong of head as he was strong of heart.

Hyde's letter about Damien made its way to Stevenson's desk, and in a fury Robert Louis Stevenson locked himself in his study and penned a 6,000 word reply that became a famous document. First published in a magazine and then as a book, Stevenson's "Open Letter to the Reverend Doctor Hyde of Honolulu" mentions that the author was entertained in Hyde's home. But, Stevenson rebukes the minister, "if you had filled me with bread when I was starving, if you had sat up to nurse my father when he lay a-dying, [your letter] would yet absolve me from the bonds of gratitude."

The accusations hurled against Damien were answered one by one. Hyde had denounced the priest as "a coarse, dirty man." "It is very possible," Stevenson remarks. "You make us sorry for the lepers who had only a coarse old peasant for their friend and father. But you, who were so refined, why were you not there to cheer them with the lights of culture?"

"We are not all," Stevenson tells Hyde, "expected to be Damiens. You having (in one huge instance) failed and Damien succeeded, I marvel it should not have occurred to you that you were doomed to silence, that when you had been outstripped in that high rivalry, and sat inglorious in the midst of your well-being, in your pleasant room —and Damien, crowned with glories and horrors, toiled and rotted in that pigsty of his under the cliffs of Kalawao—you, the elect who would not, were the last man on earth to collect and propagate gossip on the volunteer who would and did."

Hyde's reputation was marred by his slurs on Damien and by Stevenson's letter, but the minister was thoroughly discredited by a report from the district of Kohala. Hyde had accused Damien of being "not a pure man in his relations with women." Damien had worked at Kohala in the 1870's, when a priest was arrested for seducing a local woman. Damien's leprosy, according to Hyde, should therefore "be attributed to his vices and carelessness."

A report from the police in Kohala exposed the truth: a priest *had* been arrested on the island of Hawaii for sexual indecency. The priest's name, however, was not Damien. It was Fabien.

The sixteen years that Damien worked on Molokai did not, as he'd asked, remain unknown to the world. His letters to family and friends were published in England by Pamphile. The diaries, letters, and journals kept by those who'd known him were submitted to the Congregation of the

Sacred Hearts. Encyclopedias summarized Damien's life, and magazines, streets, and missionary colleges assumed his name. In Belgium, a movement gained ground to have his body returned to Louvain. The Hawaiians objected loudly. Their leper priest, they argued, had wished to stay on Molokai, on the site of the corpse tomb that he'd transformed. But in the 1930's, an agreement was reached between King Ferdinand III of Belgium and President Franklin D. Roosevelt of the United States.

On January 27, 1936, a spade plunged into the gravesite at the pandanus tree at Kalawao settlement. Bishops, priests, and nuns waited in silent prayer, and islanders again sang the farewell, "*Aloha oe.*" Damien's coffin was exhumed, covered with a Belgian flag, and transported by caisson to Mass at the cathedral in Honolulu. At dusk, it was carried aboard the American steamer, the *Republic,* sailing for San Francisco and a rendezvous at the Panama Canal. Troops marched at stopovers, and cannons boomed in salute. At the Canal, the *Republic* was met by the three-masted *Mercator* of Belgium, and Damien's coffin was lowered from one ship to the other.

On May 3, an escort of small boats preceded the *Mercator* to the dock at Antwerp. Flags waved above the expectant crowd of half a million, trumpets blared in salutation, and all the bells of the city began to peal. On the wharf was the King of Belgium and the Cardinal Archbishop of Mechlin, the princes of the kingdom and church welcoming the peasant son of Tremeloo.

A tall hearse, drawn by six white horses, brought Damien's coffin to funeral services in Antwerp. That evening the casket was conveyed to Louvain by car, passing along the farmland where, as a boy, Damien had tended sheep or dangled from the rear of market wagons, where his brother Auguste and sister Pauline had played his games of crusades and missions, and where his parents were buried. In the darkness, the moon shone on the fields of budding asparagus and on the religious shrines beside the pathways. Seventy-three years before, Damien had journeyed across the oceans to match his love against the power of death. Now the love of his countrymen had brought him to St. Joseph's Chapel at the Congregation of the Sacred Hearts. His coffin was sheltered not by the limbs of an island tree but by a man-made monument of marble. Damien the peasant priest would have appreciated the honor, yet he might well have preferred the aging, misshapen limbs of the tropical pandanus.

Leprosy remedies used most often at Kalawao settlement had come from the East—the Hoangnan pills of the Orient, the gurjun oil of the Andaman Islands, the Goto baths of Japan. In 1900, leprous patients also began swallowing or being injected with chaulmoogra oil, an extract of a shrub in India. Chaulmoogra treatments could reduce the numbers of *Mycobacterium leprae* in the body, but not on a permanent basis. Medicine had found no weapon that could combat an onslaught of the "death before death."

Finally, in the 1940's, an answer was discovered in the West. A group of drugs called sulfones was tested at the United States Public Health Hospital in Carville, Louisiana, and was proven to arrest the development of leprosy bacilli. The most common drug, Dapsone, or DDS, could halt the progression of symptoms and, after a few days or weeks of treatment, leave a patient totally noncontagious.

The death sentence was lifted. Miraculously, lepers would no longer need enforced isolation from societies of the world. After centuries, the loathsome disease could now be thwarted, halted, suspended. Dapsone was not a cure, but it eradicated *Mycobacterium leprae* in the body except in the bone marrow and liver. If treatment were maintained throughout a lifetime, Dapsone afforded a safe control of illness. Sores and ulcers healed, swelling diminished, limbs and organs functioned, disfigurement ceased. Patients who became resistant

146

to Dapsone could respond to Rifampicin, Clofazimine, or if necessary to Thalidomide, the drug that caused birth defects when used as a sedative in Europe.

Today the World Health Organization conducts regional workshops and seminars on leprosy. Patients are treated in seventy-eight control centers in forty-five countries. The organization is helping to put an end to the terror of leprosy by referring to the illness as Hansen's Disease, after Gerhard Hansen, who isolated the bacillus.

Research has uncovered new information on leprosy. The disease appears in three diagnosable forms. Tuberculoid leprosy is localized on the skin and can be self-limiting. Two more advanced stages, dimorphous—sometimes called "borderline"—and lepromatous, attack both the inner and outer body —the tissue of the muscles, organs, and nerves— and are fatal without treatment. Damien's leprosy was lepromatous.

Scientists have not yet agreed on the precise means by which the leprosy bacillus is transmitted between people. It may be airborne, or travel by insect bite, or by skin to skin contact. However, it is now certain that leprosy, or Hansen's Disease, is not highly contagious. The bacilli haven't been cultivated on artificial laboratory media, but studies of injected, slowly multiplying bacilli in the foot-pads of mice suggest that susceptibility must exist in leprous patients and that long exposure or heavy "challenge doses" are what increase the likelihood of infection.

Control projects in Burma and Thailand have calculated a sharp reduction of leprosy cases in communities where sulfone drugs are prescribed. A search continues for even more effective treatment. The nine-banded armadillo will harbor experimentally induced *Mycobacterium leprae,* and scientists hope that the animal will provide enough bacilli to allow development of an antileprosy vaccine.

At least twelve million cases of leprosy are estimated to exist in the modern world. Hospitalization, however, has become voluntary, and biopsy specimens for diagnosis are mailed to laboratory centers. In the United States, approximately 300 new cases of leprosy are tabulated each year, mostly in Louisiana, Texas, Florida, California, and New York. Few states, if any, are without one or two patients. Leprosy occurs as easily among Caucasians as among Orientals, Indians, Blacks, and Hispanics. Only the American Indian, for reasons unknown, has an immunity to the disease.

The research on leprosy was stimulated and intensified by the life example of Damien. His extraordinary martyrdom led the Catholic Church to investigate the possibility of his beatification and eventual canonization, a declaration of sainthood. Beatification would mean that Damien was venerated in a particular city, diocese, or region. Canonization, which often requires centuries of tedious survey, would bring a papal decree that Damien's name be inscribed in the book of saints and that the veneration extend to the universal Church.

The inquiry into beatification was initiated in Honolulu in the early 1890's. Bishop Koeckemann, of the Sacred Hearts Mission, was ordered to collect information on Damien's sanctity. The bishop, reluctant as always to walk in his priest's shadow, dispatched two investigators to Kalawao but supervised their report so it was understated and brief. Not until the 1930's when both Bishop Koeckemann and Léonor Fouesnel had died, did the cause for Damien's sainthood gather momentum. By then, he was firmly entrenched on the world's roster of heroes.

In 1935, formal beatification proceedings were announced in Rome. A motherhouse of the Congregation of the Sacred Hearts had been established in Rome, its archives preservin thousands of pages on Damien. The story of Damien advanced the membership in the congregation to several thousand priests and nuns, and missions were expanded to every continent. In 1967, a petition signed by 33,000 victims of leprosy in Africa, Asia, and the Americas was delivered to Pope Paul VI by the superior general of the Sacred Hearts. The petition asked for Damien's beatification, but it was not a plea from Catholic converts alone. On the list were 11,000 Hindus, 1,200 Moslems, and almost 1,000 Buddhists. Ten years later, in 1977, the pope cited Damien for his "heroic virtues," a significant step toward beatification and sainthood.

Damien's mission on Molokai ignites an interest in the entire history of the South Pacific. By 1959, when the territory of Hawaii was voted the fiftieth state of the United States, a Kalaupapa Settlement Hospital was opened and a Damien Museum was constructed in Honolulu. The Department of the Interior designated the Molokai peninsula as a national historic landmark. The main road across Kalaupapa is now Damien Boulevard, and mule tours are available to travelers on the steep curves of the *pali.* Over a hundred medically treated or discharged leper patients, now free to leave Kalaupapa, remain at the settlement. Some of these men and women were lepers before sulfone drugs became available. They exhibit more scars from their disease than anyone need suffer in the future.

The Federal law of the United States grants each state the right to place two statues of noteworthy citizens in Statuary Hall in Washington, D.C. The state of Hawaii contributed a statue of Kamehameha I, the first king of the island territory. A second statue was commissioned by a panel of judges in the mid-1960's. The sculptress Marisol Escobar created a bronze likeness of Damien de Veuster. Her work, striking in its stark originality, was unveiled at the capitol building in 1969.

Positioned among the conventional white marble of other luminaries, the statue of Damien does not show a handsome or youthful glory. Damien is depicted grimly ravaged by his leprosy. His face is swollen, his nose bulbous under the old wire spectacles. One hand is deformed. His body seems to strain to stay erect beneath the blackened bronze of its priestly cloak. But Damien has not fallen, the statue avows. He stands once again as he stood before his God, a man who could not be contained by expectations of what he should be. Damien was *what he was*. The forces within him were not at war but at one. He was stubborn, tempestuous, and impatient. He was tenderhearted, resourceful, and wise. Above all, while the religion he served de-

151

manded obedience and self-effacement, he dared to fight singlemindedly in the cause of his wretched lepers.

Most of humanity preferred to hold itself aloof from the ancient, dreaded disease of leprosy, but Damien put his faith into action, his tenderness into touch. For sixteen years, isolated on an island promontory, he embraced a forsaken colony of grotesquely ill human beings. And by his embrace, Father Damien de Veuster changed both the landscape of leprosy and the boundaries of human concern.

BIBLIOGRAPHY

Beevers, John. *The Life of Damien de Veuster, Friend of Lepers.* New York: Doubleday & Co., Inc., 1973.

Browne, S. G. "The Drug Treatment of Leprosy." *Practitioner*, October 1975, pp. 493-500.

Daws, Gavan. *Holy Man.* New York: Harper & Row, 1973.

De Veuster, Damien. *Life and Letters of Father Damien.* Edited by Father Pamphile. London: The Catholic Truth Society, 1889.

153

Dutton, Charles J. *The Samaritans of Molokai*. New York: Books for Libraries Press, 1971.

Englebert, Omer. *The Hero of Molokai*. Boston: Daughters of St. Paul, 1954.

Farrow, John. *Damien the Leper*. New York: Image Books, 1954.

Gilbert, Bil. "A Hellish Spot in Heavenly Surroundings." *Audubon*, March 1977, pp. 30-47.

Jagadisan, T. N. "Father Damien: His Life and Work." *Leprosy Review*, June 1974, pp. 170-172.

Jourdan, Vital. *The Heart of Father Damien*. Translated by Francis Larkin, S.S.C.C., and Charles Davenport. Milwaukee: The Bruce Publishing Co., 1955.

O'Connor, Richard J. "Medical Education and Training at the National Center for Hansen's Disease." United States Public Health Hospital, Carville, Louisiana.

Star, 39:1 (1979). United States Public Health Hospital, Carville, Louisiana.

Stevenson, Robert Louis. *Father Damien, An Open Letter to the Reverend Doctor Hyde of Honolulu*. New York: Cobble Hill Press, 1968.

Trautman, John R. "Treatment of Hansen's Disease." *Cutis*, July 1976, pp. 62-65.

World Health Organization. *Leprosy Control*. (WHO Chronicle, vol. 31), 1977, pp. 506-511.

World Health Organization. *Fifth Report of the Expert Committee on Leprosy* (WHO Technical Report Series, no. 607), 1977.

INDEX

156

About the Author

Anne E. Neimark was born in Chicago and attended Bryn Mawr College in Pennsylvania. She has written over two hundred stories and articles as well as several biographies for young readers. *Touch of Light, the Story of Louis Braille* won first prize for juvenile literature from the Friends of American Writers.

Mrs. Neimark is married and has three children. At present, she lives in Highland Park, Illinois.